I0955772

A PANORAMA OF SUICIDE

A PANORAMA
OF SUICIDE

A Casebook of Psychological Autopsies

By

G. DONALD NISWANDER, M.D.
Director of Psychiatric Education and Research
New Hampshire Hospital
Concord, New Hampshire

THOMAS M. CASEY, M.A.
Research Psychologist
New Hampshire Hospital
Concord, New Hampshire

and

JOHN A. HUMPHREY, Ph.D.
Assistant Professor of Sociology
The University of North Carolina
Greensboro, North Carolina

CHARLES C THOMAS · PUBLISHER
Springfield · Illinois · U.S.A.

Published and Distributed Throughout the World by

CHARLES C THOMAS • PUBLISHER

BANNERSTONE HOUSE

301-327 East Lawrence Avenue, Springfield, Illinois, U.S.A.

© 1973, by CHARLES C THOMAS • PUBLISHER

ISBN 0-398-02875-3

Library of Congress Catalog Card Number: 73-5579

With THOMAS BOOKS *careful attention is given to all details of manufacturing and design. It is the Publisher's desire to present books that are satisfactory as to their physical qualities and artistic possibilities and appropriate for their particular use.* THOMAS BOOKS *will be true to those laws of quality that assure a good name and good will.*

Library of Congress Cataloging in Publication Data

Niswander, G. Donald.
    A panorama of suicide.

    1. Suicide—Case studies. I. Casey, Thomas M., joint author.
II. Humphrey, John A., joint author.
III. Title. [DNLM: 1. Suicide. HV 6545 N727p 1973]
RC574.N57   616.8'5844   73-5579
ISBN 0-398-02875-3

Printed in the United States of America

W-1

This book is dedicated to
Our Families

ACKNOWLEDGMENTS

THIS RESEARCH WAS supported in part by a Grant from the National Institute of Mental Health.

The authors acknowledge the contributions of the following persons who were consultants to this project:

> Donna Church
> Robert LeClerc
> Donald Sanborn III
> Charlotte Perry Sanborn
> Walker Wheeler
> Whitelaw Wilson

G.D.N.
T.M.C.
J.A.H.

PROLOGUE

AT ONE TIME OR another most of us have read accounts of someone's suicide. Unlike other reports of death—car accident, drowning, heart attack, prolonged illness, or the like—the report of a suicide leaves most persons with a sense of loss and an inability to understand. Why one would take his own life remains a haunting question. If reasons or motivations are cited, they never appear to be adequate. Financial crisis, a drinking or drug problem, failing health, a jilted lover, death in the family, none of these are so unique to a given individual, that it seems suicide is the last resort.

No matter who the suicide victim is the report of his or her demise arouses our curiosity. The curiosity, even though it may be short-lived, applies to almost all suicides regardless of age, sex, religion, socio-economic status, or ethnic origin. Humans become intensely interested in someone's death by suicide which, if it came about in most any other way, would not concern us at all. At the same time, people are perplexed and even fearful of such a report. The inability to understand a suicide leads us to wonder if someone close to us would ever kill themselves. More striking, a person has the awesome thought if he is capable of killing himself. The suicide of the adolescent or young adult may be considered more tragic than that of a very old person, but interest and curiosity are aroused by both and this is generally true for the public at large.

Usually the mixture of emotions felt by the immediate family and close friends of the suicide victim may have a catastrophic impact. The blindness to the death wishes and signals given off by the victim, and the futility of efforts to prevent the tragedy, leave the survivors with intense feelings of guilt, remorse, and shame. Their intense self-condemnation and "callousness" to the deep emotional needs of the victim appear, sometimes, to bring the intended results of the suicide himself.

In some successful suicides a sigh of relief may be privately expressed by family members. The victim may have been a source of extreme hardship for the family. The ending of his life may be regarded as a situation which is beneficial for all concerned. Rarely, if ever, does one rejoice at the news of a suicide, especially that of a family member or close friend, but one source of comfort for a family may be knowing that the victim will no longer be a threat to the physical and emotional health of himself or family, or others in the community. At times suicide is almost inevitable and no surprise for some people. Frustrations by individuals close to the victim who are unable to help the victim are relieved when the end finally comes.

Nevertheless, suicide is not regarded as a quiet passing on. It has, rather, a tragic effect, probably more so than other means of death, for the family and friends of the victim.

Suicide may appear to be an unusual phenomenon to many people. Most people have not been related to or closely associated with a suicide victim. However, approximately twenty thousand people, or one in every ten thousand people, take their own life in the United States each year. Despite considerable efforts in recent years to prevent suicide, the suicide rate in this country remains fairly constant year to year, reported or otherwise.

Suicide is not rare; it is not an isolated event reserved for the mentally unbalanced; it is a major health hazard. In the past decade professionals from many related fields—psychiatrists, psychologists, sociologists, social workers, and law enforcement persons—have recognized the urgency of the problem. The quantity of scientific articles, books, and research reports on suicide indicate that there are concerned efforts being made to understand, explain, predict, and control self-destructive behavior.

All these areas of investigation about suicidal behavior tend to fall into one of three categories: 1) explanations of the variation in the rates of suicide between different societies, between different culture and sub-culture groups within a given society. These studies have tended to focus on the social structure and cultural arrangements which tend to account for differences in the suicide rate; 2) explanations of the psychological mechanisms operating within the suicidal individual. These studies have been mainly concerned with individual instances of suicidal behavior rather than the rates of such behavior; 3) studies dealing essentially with the efficacy of various methods utilized in the prevention of suicide. These have been directly concerned with crisis intervention for controlling suicidal behavior. These studies have shown considerable understanding of the conditions both external and internal to the individual which gave rise to suicidal or self-destructive behavior. On the other hand, statistical data alone, although extremely crucial in researching the problem, do not provide a view of the overall life style or history of the suicide individual.

What is lacking in the literature is an in-depth analysis of the crucial life events which lead to an individual's self-destruction. What is evident is that suicide is not the result of a few isolated events in an individual's life, but rather it is the end of a process, a process of extremely frustrating events, which pushes the individual into an irreversible decision to terminate his own life. Only a desperate individual chooses death over life. Only an individual who has, in his deliberations, reached the end of hope takes his own life.

Suicide, it is contended, results from a series of progressively frustrating events which drive the individual into increasing despair and ultimately into the firm convction that life, as he sees it, is too unbearable to continue.

As far as is known, nothing can be found in literature which presents a collection or casebook of psychological autopsies. These analyses present a complete life style of the suicide victim. It is felt that this book will provide both clinicians, researchers, and educators with case material for their use.

This book will give an account of the lives of eighteen individuals who have taken their own lives. An in-depth analysis, not only of a few factors in the individual's life, but a composite view of the life history of suicide victims should be helpful for suicidologists in the understanding, explanation, prediction, and, ultimately, in prevention of self-destructive behavior of each of the "types." Primary attention is given here to describing the context of their lives and those crucial tragedies which, in all likelihood, contributed significantly to their self-destruction.

The case histories presented in this book were compiled from the detailed social, economic, psychological, and medical information gathered for 160 completed suicides in New Hampshire during a two-year period. The anonymity of each victim is insured by disguising identifying information. In the interest of literary style, pseudonyms are used rather than initials. Hopefully, individuals and places are more than adequately protected. The data, however, is accurately presented and there are no major distortions of the individual suicide victim's life.

Suicide does occur with greater or lesser frequency between the young and the old, males and females, between the mentally ill and ostensibly normal, and the married and divorced; between the separated, widowed, and never married; the alcoholic and sober; the depressed and elated; the healthy and terminally ill. It seems to have a greater frequency in those who have suffered severe losses in their lives and in those who have been overly gratified. It can be either an impulsive act or well planned. An attempt has been made in this book to select individuals representing each of these types. In this way it is hoped to present the life-styles of a representative group of suicide victims which may be found anywhere in this country and probably the world.

Each period of life, childhood, adolescence, young adult, and old age, are included and will portray the variation in precipitating factors of suicide at different periods in an individual's life. Certainly what drives an adolescent to kill himself is considerably different from the motivation which underlies a middle-aged woman's suicide.

Most readers will know individuals who are strikingly similar to the suicide victims presented here. Normally one does not think of them as potential suicide victims. It is important to note not only the psychological characteristics of the suicide victim, but, also, their quirks or idiosyncracies and, perhaps more importantly, the nature of their social relations and, in some cases, the lack of them.

Some suicide victims have been bound intensely into social

life, whereas others have isolated themselves from any meaningful human relationship. Both of these situations are potentially depressing and dangerous, as others have pointed out, and they may ultimately lead to self-destruction.

While one may conclude in some cases that suicide was certainly predictable, given the set of circumstances which characterized the individual's life, it is also important to know why someone does not commit suicide faced with ostensibly the same frustrating situations.

The orientation of this casebook is toward the practical factors in human life which may have implications for suicide prevention or intervention. This book identifies different "types" of suicide selected from two years' data collected by the authors. "Types" must be placed in quotation marks because it is difficult to find a term that adequately describes the divisions of suicide which have been made here. There is no intended implication that a "type" of suicide is clear-cut and necessarily easily identifiable. However, there are certain commonalities in the cases presented that warrant giving certain cases a common label. It is on this basis that the "types" are presented.

It is hoped that these life histories will aid in the understanding of suicidal behavior and eventually contribute to the development of more effective suicide prevention measures.

The case histories presented in this book were collected over a two-year period from 1968-70 in New Hampshire. These data were selected from a part of a larger Federally-funded study designed to provide a clear profile of the high-risk suicidal person in the State of New Hampshire. Prior to this study no in-depth investigation of suicide had been made in this State. Not unlike the bordering states of Maine and Vermont, New Hampshire has a fairly high rate of suicide. The VITAL STATISTICS OF THE U.S., 1964, indicate that New Hampshire has the seventh highest rate of suicide in the United States (14.8 per 100,000). Only Vermont has a higher rate of suicide in New England. In New Hampshire suicide is the tenth leading cause of death. In the studies it seemed important to systematically investigate suicidal behavior in a setting characterized by high rates of such behavior. No previous studies of this nature had been done.

New Hampshire is a unique State. Its land area and population are small. The land area covers only 9,300 square miles which places it forty-fourth in the United States in size. There are 735,000 residents ranking New Hampshire forty-fifth in population size. Most of the inhabitants live in small towns ranging from less than a hundred to a few thousand people. According to the last census, the largest city, and the only Standard Metropolitan Statistical Area in the State, had 108,000 residents. There are four smaller cities with populations between 20,000 and 30,000 people. As would be expected, in the entire study it was found that the highest rates of suicide were in the small towns of the State followed by the rural areas. The few cities in New Hampshire had the lowest suicide rates of any geographic region.

Once the characteristics of the high-risk suicide population were known, attempts were made to examine the best ways of reaching and educating the high-risk group in order to make them aware of services which may become available and orient them toward using these services. The findings of this research were designed to lay the groundwork for the development of appropriate suicide intervention services.

There are twelve community mental health clinics and one center in New Hampshire located in the ten counties of the State. A professional member—psychiatrist, psychiatric social worker, or other professional social worker—of each clinic was chosen to gather data on each suicide in their region which occurred during the two year project.

Each representative was then trained in the use of the psychological autopsy. Essentially, the psychological autopsy is a multi-disciplinary approach designed to draw together and correlate medical, social, and psychiatric information about an individual before and during the final period of his life before committing suicide. Its purpose is to study the psychosocial context in which death occurs and to complement the somatic autopsy which determines the immediate cause of death. The psychological autopsy reviews the terminal phase of the patient's life against the background of his previous attitudes, life history, and modes of adaption.[1]

With respect to suicide, Shneidman *et al.*,[2] have amply demonstrated the value of the psychological autopsy and the "death investigation team" in the study of suicide. As they conceived it, the primary purpose of the psychological autopsy is to establish the intention and lethality of people who are the victims of accident, illness, poisonings, other fatalities, and obvious suicide. By interviewing families, acquaintances of the deceased, and reconstructing the life-style of the victim, their death investigation team sought to clarify the degree to which a victim participated in bringing about his own death. The psychological autopsy then is a method of data collection providing a structural interview schedule which reconstructs the life history of the deceased focusing upon the period just prior to death. The data include: "every available observation, fact, and opinion about a recently deceased person in an effort to understand the psycho-social components of death."

Specifically, the version of the psychological autopsy used in this study included sixteen sections:

1) Identifying information, i.e. the victim's name, date of birth, place of birth, race, religion, time and place of death, physical description, marital status, surviving members of immediate family, living arrangements, address and type of domicile.

2) Details of death, including method, time, place, etc.

3. Outline of victim's history: the social history of the victim is investigated in great detail.

4) Death history: focuses on relatives and family members who have died and the cause of death.

5) Personality and life style.

6) Reaction to disequilibrium.

7) Triggering of suicide.

8) Role of alcohol, drugs, and depression.

---

[1] Wiseman, A. D., Kastenbaum, R.: *The Psychological Autopsy, A Study of the Terminal Phase of Life.* CMH Monograph No. 4, 1968.

[2] Farberow, N. L., and Shneidman, E. (eds.): *The Cry for Help.* New York, McGraw Hill, 1961.

9) Identity.
10) Premonitions or fears.
11) Changes: social, economic, psychological.
12) Life side of victim.
13) Intention.
14) Lethality of suicide attempt.
15) Informants.
16) Comment.

CONTENTS

A PANORAMA OF SUICIDE

In considering the cases of suicide, the reader should note that each case is followed by an abstract. For each category "type" of suicide there are two case studies except for The Minimum Signal Suicide "type" where only one case study was found. The cases are followed by comments on the type of suicide and on the cases themselves.

1

CHILD AND ADOLESCENT SUICIDE

PSYCHOLOGICAL AUTOPSY ON
HERMAN FARNSWORTH

H ERMAN FARNSWORTH WAS A sixteen-year old white Protestant at the time of his death. He was the youngest and only child living at home with his mother and father on a dilapidated farm on the outskirts of a small town with a population of 1,000. He would have completed his sophomore year in high school in June 1968. He was employed several hours a week after school and on Saturdays at a local market. At the same time, he helped his parents with their vegetable garden and helped take care of his father's game cocks. His five elder siblings, three males and two females, were all married and lived outside the community. He was known as "Pete" to his family and always referred to his father by his first name, Ralph, although he called his mother "Mom."

This family had always been poor yet managed to live on their own meager means. They were ostracized in the community to which Mr. Farnsworth counteracted by ostracizing it. His father was generally known in the community as an "eccentric old bastard" who farmed, raised and showed reptiles at fairs, and wrote papers and gave speeches at various gatherings about reptiles. He also raised some game cocks which he entered in cock fights. He had several champions. Herman's mother had held various housekeeping jobs and was employed on a regular daily basis at the time of Herman's death. She was out of the home working most of the time.

The family had lived on this farm for twenty-one years. The property was overgrown with brush except for a neat garden at the rear; the front yard was a maze of various kinds of home-made cages containing several varieties of fowl. The house itself was a weather-worn frame one and barely recognizable as a residence. Glass windows were few and there were several makeshift patched screens for protection. Extending to the

5

rear of the house were several shed additions all attached to one another. These contained an incredible amount of litter of scrap metal, wood, etc. Mr. Farnsworth boastfully reported that fourteen artists had done paintings of his house. One of them commented that it was "out of this world" which delighted him.

Herman was a full-term baby delivered by Cesarean section. At the time of Herman's birth, the Department of Public Welfare was involved with this family investigating complaints of child neglect and abuse with reference to the home and the reptiles. No action resulted but Mr. Farnsworth continued to be very bitter about this.

Herman was described as no different as a child from his older brothers, nineteen years, seventeen years, and nine years his senior; and sisters, thirteen years, and four years his senior. He was good friends with the eldest brother but this dropped off when the brother married; Herman did not like his wife. All of the siblings had left the home as soon as they graduated from high school. For the most part, the children shunned their parents and there were frequent angry outbursts. At the time of Herman's death, they would have nothing to do with the parents at all. The parents stated they had brought their children up "a little different" from the manner of other parents.

Herman "never kicked" about going to school and was an average student in achievement. He never brought home books to study nor missed attending school except when the parents kept him home to help on the farm several days a year. During his last year he had taken cooking at school because he did not care for the shop teacher. He was very interested in cooking, baking pastries, and preparing meals at home.

When Herman was twelve years old, his father suffered a severe heart attack and was immobilized for a year. After that he could sit outside and direct the work of the farm, most of which was done by Herman. In addition, the year before his death Herman helped to pick as many as eighteen hundred quarts of blueberries; he hated the job.

Herman was very ambitious working the farm and also helping neighbors after he was ten or twelve years old. In the past two years before he died, he had held paying jobs caring for neighbors' horses, haying, planting, and the like. He opened a savings account and kept his bankbook on a special hook in his room. A week before his death he had unsuccessfully tried to give his $300 in savings to his father.

Herman's general physical health was very good although he often took aspirin for an unknown reason. He had frequent nosebleeds. He did not smoke or drink. A doctor's attention was sought only three times in his life, the last being four days before his death when he could not get up in the morning and seemed physically exhausted and ill. He had been having trouble sleeping for about six weeks. During the past year he became very close to a nearby family whose means were strikingly better and in whose yard he killed himself. They had a neat frame home which gave a solid middle class effect. They had known Herman for years as a neighborhood youngster but became much more acquainted a year before his death when Herman became friends with their eldest son, a boy his age. The boys built a shooting range behind the friend's home where they often practiced. This relationship dropped off in January of 1968, five months before Herman died, as his friend was far more popular; but Herman continued to frequent their home and was welcome. Here he helped the housewife around the house, sometimes preparing full course meals as a surprise if the family was otherwise occupied at the dinner hour. He became very attached to this woman, a warm and attractive person. Although he target shot with the father and son, Herman spent more and more time around her, singling her out; he even criticized her son to his mother for not doing more for her. She handled this by saying she enjoyed doing what she did. At one point when she had joined the neighborhood boys to jog around the block, Herman called her late that night, angry that she had not jogged with him that day because he had waited for her. The father and a minister were later involved in trying to help Herman handle his infatuation with his wife.

This more-or-less adopted family felt sorry for Herman's plight at home and a year before his death criticized his parents for not encouraging him to enter into teenage activities. Herman's parents relented and allowed him to join the church youth group. Herman stopped going without explanation after several weeks; his father was a proclaimed atheist.

Herman was never known to fight and was considered a very thoughtful, good, and kind-hearted boy. He was sometimes looked down upon by peers for his withdrawing behavior but held no hatred for either them or his family, although the latter was usually the reason for his being shunned. He was not known to cry but frequently looked sad, especially in a peer group.

Herman was extremely well thought of by adults. He was industrious and polite. His father fostered relationships with adults for its educational purpose—"education is more important than money" and because "all he would learn from kids was about marijuana and dope." The father allowed that Herman was the only one of his children with whom he could get along and described him as "the kind of boy you dream about but never see." On the other hand, he criticized Herman for being interested only in television and guns.

Herman seldom joined in with the other children in the neighborhood or school. He felt different and unliked. During the two years before he died, although he was invited to parties or sporting events, he seldom went believing he was not really wanted. He was often seen sitting alone on a fence or at the sidelines of neighborhood ice hockey. He had a talent as an ice hockey goalee but refused to try for the school team.

When someone close to Herman was under stress (and he sometimes read stress where there was none) he made every attempt to help them, usually through some form of work. He kept his own feelings inside for the most part and took things out on himself. He would withdraw, isolate himself, and blame himself for any sort of trouble; he was also a worrier. Sometimes he confronted others if he did not understand what was expected or a point in discussion. He spoke of killing himself both to his own family and to the neighbor family because he felt incapable of accomplishing anything; the month before his death, he felt unwanted.

Herman had been working very hard on his parents' farm since the spring of his death in addition to his schoolwork and his part-time job. He was very tired, looked pale, and began falling asleep occasionally at the neighbors' house where he frequently had dinner. Ten days before his death he skipped school and arrived at the neighbors' house in the morning. He told his friend's mother that they had "games to play" meaning him and her. She was alone at the time and they sat down in her living room. She asked just what the matter was with him. He then went to one of the bedrooms and came out with a gun which he had apparently come in and left there without her noticing. Herman told her of his affection for her and that he was going to kill himself. She got the gun away from him by telling him he knew she couldn't force him to give it to her. She explained that she understood his feelings; she told him that she herself had been attracted to older persons of the opposite sex when she was young. On the pretense of calling her employer, she telephoned the local minister who arrived soon after and talked with Herman and made an appointment for the following day to see him again. In the meantime, the clergyman went to a private psychologist to discuss Herman's situation and intentions. The family physician was also notified and planned to see Herman. He did not keep the appointment with the minister the following day.

There was nothing unusual noted the weekend prior to his death. At the first of the week, Herman was driving the family truck with his father and he swung too wide on a corner skidding into a ditch. He commented that he guessed he hadn't learned how to turn corners well. His father replied, "That's evident." The father wondered if there might not have been something wrong with his eyes. The next day his mother noticed that Herman's bankbook was not in the customary place and she had found it along with his pistol together with a note in his drawer saying that he intended to kill himself. The parents did not know what to do but the father finally decided to call and ask Herman to bring some special fish home from the market which he did in late afternoon. Although he had not been marked absent, he "skipped" school the next morning. He went to the neighbors with his own rifle. He said he was afraid he could never come to the house again because of his feelings for the housewife and feared her husband's retaliation. At this point the minister was called again and Herman agreed to see the family physician. The minister talked alone with Herman and confronted him with his "fixation" on the mother of his friend.

The next day Herman could not get up in the morning and the family physician was called. He was very concerned about Herman and made an appointment to see him again a week later, a day after his death. At the time the physician planned to have Herman see a colleague clinical psychologist at the same clinic.

Herman attended school and worked as usual for the rest of the week before his death. On the weekend he went to pick up his neighbor's Model #8 Remington as a target shooting was planned the next morning. When he left their home they kidded him about at least letting them sleep until 7:00 a.m.

Herman customarily rose at 5:00 a.m. but had been having trouble sleeping the past few weeks prior to his death. He got up a little earlier the day he died as he had for the past few days. He met his father in the kitchen that morning, who asked Herman if he wanted some coffee. Herman accepted and they sat in the dining room—living room combination together. Herman told his father that he felt "real bad" to which his father replied philosophically that "life was anticipation." His father told Herman that he would have to "find his way;" his father admitted that he could not help him. Herman left shortly thereafter.

Two hours later the father received a telephone call to go to the neighbors' house because Herman had shot himself. The neighbors' house was on the main highway about a quarter mile through fields and woods behind the farm owned by Herman's family.

The neighbors later said they heard a shot shortly after arising. A little later, the housewife saw Herman coming through the field several hundred feet behind the house. She knew that

Herman had been feeling upset lately and went out to talk with him. He was fully clothed and looked very pale and strained. He was carrying the gun which he had borrowed from them the previous night. He sat down against a haystack and they talked for several minutes. Herman was despondent because he felt his father did not care for him, that no one liked him—even this neighboring family. She tried to persuade him to go and play with her eldest son and she also tried to reassure him that their family cared for him. She was somewhat frustrated and felt helpless with Herman, which she thought he sensed, because he told her she was still the most wonderful person in the world. She then tried to get him to come into the house to have breakfast; when he refused, she stood up with the unverbalized intention of getting her husband to come and talk with Herman. She had taken several steps when she heard a shot, ran back and saw he had pointed the gun muzzle under his chin and pulled the trigger.

There are contradictory reports on Herman's last statements before killing himself. A clergyman reported the neighbor as saying Herman said his father told him, "If you are going to kill yourself, then go and do it." His father said nothing about a discussion of suicide having taken place that morning. He commented that there was one thing he had to see about Herman —his physicial position at death and he added, "If he learned nothing else from me, he did what I said, 'It's better to die on your feet than live on your knees.'"

Herman obviously felt very hopeless the morning of his death; his suicide did seem definitely intentional. For two weeks he had left numerous clues and told no less than three people of his intention to kill himself with the apparent hope he would find rescue. He had already fired one shot on the day of his death and talked with the neighbor's wife for several minutes following a rejectional conversation with his father. He felt let down by his father and was encouraged to kill himself if his father did say, in fact, "Go ahead and get it over with," as reported. It is probable that Herman interpreted the housewife's frustration and going to her husband as rejection. This was the final loss of esteemed objects. These sequential factors combined to balance his intention toward the direction of suicide.

HERMAN FARNSWORTH

A picture of sadness and deprivation best characterize this young man. His life was one of hardship and rejection by his parents. He lived in a ramshackle house on meagre means.

The family had been investigated on the grounds of child neglect at the time of his birth. Herman was an industrious boy who worked on the family farm plus the neighbors', and at odd jobs to keep the family going.

It is little wonder he became attached to a neighboring woman, the mother of one of his friends; she was warm and kindhearted. Very likely beneath the veneer of industry and politeness lay a great deal of parental hostility. He was socially withdrawn, by his own choice, and partially by the demands of his parents. His anger was inner-directed; he blamed himself for anything that went wrong. Herman is almost the paradigm of the suicidal adolescent. He had so little support and nothing to live for.

PSYCHOLOGICAL AUTOPSY ON
HOWARD JESSOP

Howard Jessop was only fifteen when he committed suicide by hanging himself. He was the third child in a family of five. An infant sibling died but two sisters and a brother were still living as were his parents. Howard was born in northern New England and lived there all his life.

Two markedly different pictures of this boy are given—one by his mother and one by his school principal and guidance counselor. Mrs. Jessop was quite defensive when relating Howard's background. She described him as never sad, never unhappy, and further emphasized that one of his misfortunes was that his school teachers didn't understand him. Mrs. Jessop further related that her son was very sorry for the less fortunate. She told in some detail about his "close and sharing" relationship with a blind classmate. The mother identified Howard's sensitivity with her own.

Mr. Jessop was a laborer in the construction business. He was generally laid off during the winter months when he worked in the woods. The father had a saw mill in back of the barn where he and Howard worked together. According to Mrs. Jessop, Howard was somewhat frightened of his father, who, at times, could be quite harsh. In one of the interviews with Mrs. Jessop, her husband came in and was obviously intoxicated. He was uncooperative and even hostile toward the interviewer. His only contribution to the conversation was that Howard was quick-tempered and impulsive; for example, he related an incident of two or three months previously when Howard had hit a friend on a shoulder then grabbed him apologetically.

Mrs. Jessop said her husband, because of the nature of his work, had always been out of the home a great deal. Two years before Howard's death, he was home more frequently because

13

there were construction projects in the immediate area where he had employment. At one point Mr. Jessop left home for approximately four months. During this time Mrs. Jessop reportedly had male companions. This rather informal separation was probably provoked by Mr. Jessop's drinking. At the same time the eldest daughter became pregnant and later married a young man who was not the father of her child. In the Spring the father went to the Jessop home and threatened to remove the girl in spite of her mother's protestations. At the same time Howard got more involved with the same family becoming friendly with the blind son; also another Jessop daughter began dating one of the sons in the same family.

Howard's school principal said that his behavior was "generally aggravating." He talked back to his teachers, threw chalk, and smoked where it was not permitted. As a result, he angered many of his teachers and the school administration. He was placed in the "slow" group. His I.Q. on his Otis Beta testing in May of 1964 revealed a score of sixty-nine, while in 1967 he achieved a score of ninety-four; a reading problem was discovered but never treated. He was kept back in the second grade but then he advanced normally although social deprivations were obviously deterring to his development.

During the Fall before his death, Howard had frequent detentions (staying after school) because of his behavior. On the day of his death he refused any more restrictions and threatened the principal that he would never come back to school. At this point the principal contacted his mother to arrange for a conference the following Monday.

Following the suicide, a school guidance counselor was interviewed and he felt there was a good deal of pathology in the family with a great capacity for acting out behavior. For example, following Howard's death a sister had been truant frequently and this was interpreted as her dropping out. Howard's brother had been a problem in school for some time and some of his behavior was extremely sadistic, such as burning children behind the ear with cigarette butts. Again, following Howard's death, this brother had taken to racing his car up and down the main street of the town and being truant from school.

In addition, the guidance counselor felt that none of the family members were close to one another emotionally, although the brother frequently said he and Howard were "soul mates."

The concluding paragraph of the guidance counselor's report said he had known Howard for only two months and enjoyed talking with him. Howard seemed interested at times in his education and was curious about his difficulty in learning to read. Howard prided himself on his practical knowledge of machinery, animal husbandry, and farm life, but was completely at sea at school mainly because of reading difficulty.

The counselor felt frustrated that the school did not have a remedial reading teacher. He also sympathized with inexperienced faculty members who sometimes found Howard to be a discipline problem. The counselor felt that his behavior was immature and similar to that of several of his friends. In his opinion, Howard enjoyed the constant attention of his peers and acted foolish occasionally for their attention. This trained professional felt that he was of average intelligence despite the results of the psychological tests. It was his impression that Howard had a desire to live.

Following the suicide, Howard's minister was also contacted. He saw Howard and his family as a tragedy. Mr. Jessop had not allowed Howard to participate in church affairs for the past six months since the boy was needed to work around the farm. The minister had several conferences with the family in an attempt to encourage them to allow Howard and his sister to attend church-related activities. These efforts met with little success. He felt that Howard had many fine qualities, although he recognized that Howard was somewhat hyperactive and also supersensitive about his school failures over the years. A few months before Howard's death, he found him doing quite well in the church group activities; he related well to others and was eager to please and to be helpful toward both the minister and his wife. The minister made the comment that Howard seemed to him and his wife as his "giving parents."

In mid-winter Howard committed sucide by hanging himself

in the barn located in the back of the family home in a rural section of New Hampshire. That very day Howard had been sent to the principal's office because of his flippancy toward a teacher with whom he had a good relationship previously. At this point the principal became quite upset with Howard because of the chronicity of complaints about his behavior. He threatened Howard with exclusion from school if his behavior did not improve. Before Howard went home by the school bus, the principal discussed the situation with Mrs. Jessop and they planned a conference the following week. Needless to say, that conference never took place.

The family noted that during the last three or four days of Howard's life, he went to bed much earlier than usual and also talked in his sleep. He always gritted his teeth while sleeping; his mother related this to school difficulties.

Howard apparently committed suicide in an impulsive, angry fashion as a result of family, school, and social problems. He grew up in a home lacking emotional warmth and nurturance and had been exposed to a high degree of acting out on all levels by his father and mother. Educational achievement was secondary to survival. His family was not accepted by other members of the community; significantly, the family's affect was quite flat, whereas the school's and church's concern were much more appropriate and involved. Nevertheless, neither of the latter groups were able to provide Howard with the type of support which might have sustained his life.

HOWARD JESSOP

Howard was fifteen when he committed suicide, the final tragedy of his life. The apparent triggering event was his being sent to the principal of his school for some wrongdoing in the classroom. The principal's call to Howard's mother prompted her to send Howard into the house when he arrived home that afternoon.

In retrospect, something was awry in Howard's life shortly prior to his suicide. He had gone to bed earlier than usual and had talked in his sleep. On the afternoon shortly before his death, Howard said he would rather die than go back to school: this bad a threat did it pose to him. Thus he had shaped his own demise though no one apparently paid much, if any, attention to him.

His school had been especially frustrating since Howard was a slow learner as defined by the school. That frustration, and his being barred from social participation, and the lack of a warm home-life were seemingly contributing factors to his suicide. Whatever caused it, Howard hanged himself in his last final act.

The Child and Adolescent Suicide

Suicide in adolescents is a relatively rare occurrence. In fact, some authors are of the opinion that suicide, as we know it, cannot occur in children under the age of eleven. This is not to say that these young people cannot be partially responsible for their own deaths by suicide but the major burden of responsibility lies elsewhere. The mind of a child is not sufficiently developed to be able to plan and conceive the act of self-destruction and its finality. Moreover, it is felt that there is not sufficient reasoning power to plan the act such that detection and intervention will not take place particularly in persons younger than eleven. To some investigators this may be a moot point, but childhood suicide has been considered as not happening below the age of eleven.

There is a particular reason for placing children's and adolescents' suicides in a separate category. It is true that they would ordinarily be classified under other types of suicide (for example under impulsive), but that would not call proper attention to the problem of childhood suicide. Moreover, children's suicides are qualitatively different and especially tragic. They are deserving of special analysis geared toward crisis intervention.

Perhaps the most striking similarity between Herman and Howard is the fact that they both came from such emotionally and financially deprived backgrounds and from farms. Both boys were almost "licked before they got started," so to speak. Both families were fraught with pathology. Of the two, probably Herman had the happier life and, however marginal, was better adjusted.

From the time of his birth Herman was fated toward an unhappy existence. He was born into, and had to live with, privation. Socially he and his family were ostracized because of their poverty and peculiar manners. Because she worked, Herman's mother was not at home much of the time. His father was anything but an understanding man. However, Herman had a number of qualities going for him. For one thing, he was industrious and ambitious since he worked not only on his father's farm but also for the neighbors. Herman, unlike Howard, was able to form a sound and trusting relationship with one of the older women in the neighborhood. Howard apparently had few or no close relations either within or outside his family. Both boys had a great deal of hostility; Howard showed his hostility more than Herman. It was this very hostility that proved to be the boys' undoing since the anger became retroflexed and introverted resulting in suicide.

Howard appeared unable to demonstrate his emotions toward anyone while Herman was able to relate to the neighbor's wife. For Herman, when his trusting relationship was broken, everything seemed hopeless to him and he did not want to live any longer.

In children and adolescents the concept of suicide is somewhat different from that held by adults. For a child suicide probably means the cessation of physical or mental pain without any realization that the stopping is permanent. For adolescents there may be some realization of the finality of suicide; self-destructive behavior is more likely the result of immature impulsive behavior. It is unlikely that they perceive the full ramifications of their actions. This was undoubtedly true in both Herman's and Howard's cases. Just how much they realized the finality of their acts cannot really be stated though it seems that they were quite aware of what they were doing.

As can be seen from the case summaries, both boys have strikingly similar backgrounds. Of course it would be unwise to attempt to generalize from these two cases but it is of interest that suicide among adults occurs more frequently in the farm population. It might be that similar forces are at work to act on both children and adults.

This analysis will raise more questions than can be answered in this short space. Of course the reason is that suicide in children is such a futile and tragic occurrence, particularly when signs and signals as described in both of the psychological autopsies go unheeded. Very possibly both Herman and Howard might be living and contributing to the social environment for which they both showed some potential.

2

THE IMPULSIVE SUICIDE

PSYCHOLOGICAL AUTOPSY ON THEODORE CROFT

T HEODORE CROFT WAS twenty-two, white, and of no religious affiliation when he decided he did not want to live any longer. He was born in a small New England town and was the third of ten children; he had seven brothers and two sisters. As the family described him, Ted was apparently closer to his mother than to his father.

His father was a self-employed mason for a great many years. Although he had the closer attachment to his mother, Ted didn't seem to mind being told what to do by his brothers or father; but he disliked authority from other sources. He dropped out of school in the ninth grade. After this he held a variety of unskilled jobs. Ted appeared to be a jolly person who didn't seem to let anything bother him. Not much else could be found about the early life of this young man. It was the impression that he was somehow "lost in the shuffle" of a family of ten children.

In 1964 he became involved in a series of mostly petty criminal offenses such as drunk and disorderly conduct, petty larceny, and alcohol infractions. He was arrested thirty-one times and served seven months at a house of correction during that year. Prior to his marriage in 1965 he had been arrested seven times. His wife was pregnant at the time of their marriage.

If someone gave Ted a hard time while he was drinking, he would frequently counteract. Still his police encounters were explained by the family as "doing a few little things." The family felt the police were down on him and hounded him. One of his brothers felt the police caused his death.

One example of the distorted family value system is conveyed in this example: he was prohibited by the police from entering a local cafe. Shortly after this prohibition he entered the cafe with a friend. The friend drank some beer but Ted drank nothing. The proprietor called the police who proceeded to throw Ted out. In the course of this confrontation he hit the police officer. The family felt this example showed the police were picking on Ted because "he wasn't doing anything to bother anyone there." The fact Ted had been prohibited from going there didn't mean a thing. Ted felt this was discriminatory and unfair. According to the family, the police "pressed him and pressed him hard." The police made him mad because he didn't like to be pushed. One police official openly expressed that Ted's death was no loss to the community.

The family reported they rarely heard anything unkind about Ted. Ted was not a "loner." He enjoyed the company of others, always seemed happy, and had a way of cheering others up. People liked him on first meeting and afterwards; children liked him very much. However, he was basically impulsive. He rarely planned ahead in any of his endeavors. His life had a quality of immediacy and he lived in and for the present. He didn't seem to care whether he held a job or not. He always had bills to pay but they usually were no greater at the end of one job than at the beginning. He held jobs for short periods of time, usually for only a few weeks. His family felt that Ted just didn't like working. He spent a great deal of his leisure time riding around in a car. He especially enjoyed playing pool, fishing, and hunting, although he never owned a gun.

In the spring of 1967 he suddenly went to Florida hoping "to get away from the people up here." His wife and their three children, aged three, two, and three months eventually joined him. Nothing is known of their life there but in the spring of 1968 they returned to New Hampshire. Ted had to borrow the money from his in-laws to get back home. After this return and until his death, he held three different jobs as an unskilled laborer.

Ted's marriage did not work out well. When he went to the house of correction for one of the larceny charges, his wife received welfare. When she started receiving this aid, she had vowed never to see him again. She began seeing other men but Ted didn't find out until the night of his death. Her actions greatly upset him. He felt very lonely because his wife had abandoned him. At the same time a court appearance for non-support indicates that he must have abandoned her also. A family member said she was much more important to him than he was to her.

When Ted was released from jail the last time, he went to live with his mother. One brother asked him to go on a fishing trip; Ted agreed and his brother said, "Aren't you going to ask your wife?" Ted replied, "What for, it wouldn't make any difference."

On the day of Ted's death, his wife called to say she would take him back. However, when he went to see her shortly after she called, she wasn't at home and he somehow found out that she had left with a man. He returned to his mother's home. Then a brother-in-law accompanied him to look for his wife at various nearby locations. This search was without success and he returned to his mother's house. His mother and a sister each retired for the night after the children were in bed. His brother-in-law stayed up with him until almost midnight when the brother-in-law went to bed. He left Ted alone in the kitchen supposedly getting ready to go to work.

Just twenty minutes later there was a shot and the brother-in-law ran to the kitchen where he found Ted collapsed over a 16-gauge shotgun. There was a gaping wound in his stomach. A police ambulance was called; Ted was pronounced dead on arrival at the city hospital.

No fear of death, accidents, or suicidal thinking were reported by the family. In many ways Ted's life was a paradox. He hid behind the facade of a happy, jolly person. He internalized his stressful feelings. Conversely, his acting-out patterns are shown by his thirty-one arrests and his search for his wife. How is one to interpret the paradox which Theodore Croft left as his unhappy bequest?

THEODORE CROFT

Ted Croft led an impoverished life. He came from a large family. In spite of this he had no one with whom to identify or turn to when he was in trouble. Ted was antisocial; he had many encounters with the law although mostly for petty reasons. At this time he was earning the reputation of being a "bad risk."

One night he could not find his wife. She had offered reconciliation but that simply was something he did not understand. He fell silent even though he found out she would have him back. This was not enough of a boost to pull him away from his feelings. One by one his family went to bed the night of his death; no one seemed to perceive all the losses that Ted had undergone.

PSYCHOLOGICAL AUTOPSY ON ALBERT BOYD

Albert Boyd was born twenty years ago in a small New England town as the sixth of ten children. He completed the eighth grade and left school to begin work. His school years were unremarkable; his grades were average and his boyhood hobbies were rearing rabbits, hunting, and working in his garden. It was said, however, his home was impoverished; it is doubtful that either of his parents could read.

In spite of this possible illiteracy, his parents described Albert as a boy who minded well, seldom talked back, and who was very cooperative within the family unit. But they did add that he had a flashing temper and was quick to fight. The police in his community felt he was one of a number of young men "to keep an eye on," but Albert was not an outright troublemaker.

Following his leaving school, his first job was with a manufacturing concern as an unskilled laborer. This job only lasted two months; Albert left simply because he was dissatisfied. Shortly after that he got a similar type job where he stayed for one and a half years. Since he was approaching draft age, he left this employment to enlist in the armed service in 1968. A few months prior to his enlistment, a sister attempted suicide. Details were lacking about this incident since the family refused to discuss the matter.

Little is known about Albert's initial service adjustment but he came home on leave proud to be a member of the armed services. His leave was enjoyed by both him and his family. When it came time to return to his base, a New England "nor'easter" snowed for three days. All air travel was cancelled during this period. He was already late in returning to his base command. Finally he was able to take a flight from a nearby city to New York that would take him to the west, his next station. At the travel outset, and unnoticed by Albert, the flight ticket agent on the first leg of the flight took the portion of his ticket from New York to the west. Consequently, when he got to New York he could not board his scheduled plane westwardly. His belongings flew along to the west but he had to return home. Adjustments were reassured him by the airline when he returned home but they were not immediately forthcoming and would have cost twice the original estimations by the airline. Back at home he didn't want to return to the base, although his father said he was willing to borrow the necessary money. His mother called the Red Cross and she was told that Albert should turn himself in at the nearest Red Cross office. He did not heed this advice.

Since his absence from the armed services coincided with holidays, he looked forward to and participated in the family Christmas. Albert alternated between saying he would go back and "I'll wait until the MP's come and get me." On the other hand, he increasingly made the statement, "If they come after me, I'll kill myself." His greatest spoken fear was a military stockade in which he would be confined for his over-leave. At other times he told his mother and father he would serve his time, whatever it was, and then return home. But most of all he worried about incarceration in the stockade.

His vacillating statements about serving his time whatever it might be and his wanting to go out and kill himself reached a peak on the night before he committed suicide. He was talking of killing himself; his parents stayed up trying to reason with him until the mid-early morning. During this time he repeatedly expressed his fear of the military stockade. The parents finally got him calmed down so that at the mid-morning hour all of them could go to sleep.

At nine o'clock the same morning, the local Chief of Police received a call from Albert's father stating his son was AWOL from the service and he wanted to turn him in. In an hour the Chief arrived at the Boyd's home. He spoke briefly to Mr. Boyd who then called Albert downstairs; Albert had isolated himself from the rest of the household. The Chief, who was an ex-serviceman, knew the distinction between picking up someone who was AWOL and having a serviceman turn himself in. Therefore, he asked Albert, "Is that right? You want to turn yourself in?" Albert replied, "Yes."

The Chief asked for his military orders. Albert went upstairs, got them, and returned. At this point the Chief called the military police in Boston and then made a call to a nearby police station to see if they had facilities to hold the boy until the military police from Boston arrived to pick him up.

While the Chief was on the phone, Albert asked his father if he could go upstairs again. The father at first said, "No." When his son said he had to go to the bathroom, the father gave permission. Within a minute a shot was heard and the Chief ran upstairs. Albert was found on the floor near the door inside his bedroom. A .22 caliber automatic rifle was on his bed nearby.

His mother, in another second floor room, came immediately and offered her assistance where police were giving first aid. The father was so emotional and erratic that he never went to the second floor. Local medical assistance was summoned. But Albert died within a few minutes having a bullet wound in the center of his heart.

The Chief of Police said later that had he not been in the house at the time, he would have found it extremely difficult to believe it was a suicide because Albert did not impress him as the type of young man who would kill himself. Albert was not at all anxious and he seemed perfectly calm and collected when he went upstairs and killed himself. On the other hand, Albert's father knew immediately what had happened when he heard the shot and he could not bring himself to go upstairs; he became disorganized and unable to function. Afterwards the mother became the "rock" for the family to lean on, giving her strength to them.

Albert was buried with military honors.

ALBERT BOYD

Albert Boyd's enemy was fear and a realistic fear. He was
accidentally Absent Without Leave from the military service
and he feared punishment for this. He had been pretty much
on his own all his life and, when the service let him down in
assisting his return to his base, he simply could not deal with
the possible rebuke, dishonor, and disgrace. Albert's adjustment
to this plight was psychologically primitively impulsive and
suicide must have seemed the only way out. His family was
supportive to him but they were unable to read his "cry for help."

The Impulsive Suicide

Like most impulsive behaviors, the impulsive act of self-
destruction is an enigma. In the case of suicide, the act is
especially difficult to explain. The illustrations of Theodore
Croft and Albert Boyd present a bleak, sparse picture, not only
in terms of their life style, but with regard to the amount of
information available. Both these men were in their twenties,
one was in trouble with the local law enforcement agency; the
other, with the military. Both faced confinement.

Albert and Ted both came from large impoverished families.
As far as could be determined but not clearly stated in the case
reports, one would assume their initial adaptation to life was
primitive and had to be on a "moment to moment" basis.

Both men were emotionally immature. Ted, unfortunately,
turned to a life of petty crime; Albert was able to contain himself
to a "flashing temper." Albert was able to channel his energies
into joining the armed forces. This outlet was not open to Ted
because of his police record.

Albert's service connection may have served as a deterrent
to his getting married. Ted's marriage and adjustment was
marginal and eventually it turned out to be disastrous. In both
instances the one major step that both of these suicides took
indirectly led to their eventual demise. Although Albert was
proud to be a member of the armed services, he was still terrified
to turn himself over to the military authorities for an obvious
deep fear of being punished. While the probability of this fear

was realistic, it hardly seemed sufficient to be the cause of his suicide. Ted's marriage was beset by innumerable difficulties and, when he could not find his wife at a crucial point, he saw fit to take his own life.

There are a number of explanations which might shed some light on why these young men committed suicide. None of these appear to supply reasons which are entirely sufficient. One can say these young men had no one with whom to identify strongly during the critical adolescent years as far as could be determined in gathering the psychological autopsy data. Therefore, there was no one on whom they could rely in later life during times of crisis. This is very probably true of many individuals of the working class but they do not end up as suicides in crisis situations. Apart from individual identification, there was little in the way of group identification for either Albert or Ted. Both seemed to be "loners." Still, the same holds true for many other individuals who do not commit suicide. What was peculiar to Albert and Ted that led them to this unhappy decision?

One thing they had in common was that they both came from large families in which each could lose themselves easily and seem almost as strangers to the rest of the family in each home. This gave each little or nothing which each could call his own. When each finally got something of his own and it was threatened in one way or another, each reacted out of proportion to the possible loss. Ted thought he finally possessed something that was his and his alone, namely his wife. When that possession was threatened, he was unable to face life. Albert was threatened apparently by something he had never before experienced; the threat of dishonor and disgrace was something he could not face.

Both Albert and Ted were almost compelled to take care of themselves. Coming from such impoverished homes and families, they had to take the initiative whenever they wanted something done. Ted's family support took the form of their defending his petty criminal acts. He was unable to accept these rather transparent defenses. Albert did not know how to accept help from his father in order to pay for an airplane ticket which might have removed his fear from punishment by reason of his being able to return to his base. In any event, both had to fend for themselves without very much assistance. When placed in an intolerable situation, they simply were not equipped to handle the problems when confronted with the situations.

Since neither had been taught socially acceptable "ways out" of difficult situations, their primitive training apparently led them to suicide as an ultimate solution. If Ted had other psychological resources, he would at least have had someplace to turn when he was unable to locate his wife.

Other solutions might have been for Albert to contact the base of his new assignment and explain the circumstances which beset him. While this might not have solved everything, it surely would have done no harm.

Neither man was sufficiently well-trained to handle intense anger in a constructive manner. They both were fearful and unable to foresee the consequences of their actions. Emotionally they might be considered "grown" adolescents who could not realize that a temporary delay might make a tremendous difference to them. If Ted were unable to reconcile with his wife, he might well have found alternative means of satisfaction.

The roots of both of their problems probably lay mainly in their social impoverishment. Neither had very much and when what they did have was threatened, it resulted in their suicides.

With regard to the particulars of each case, one may wonder why Ted, who had committed so many anti-social acts, decided to turn his aggression against himself. On thirty-one occasions that we know he made some offense against society. Indirectly he harmed himself, although it did not seem to bother him. When it came to his wife, he harmed himself directly and lethally. In doing so he harmed others but it seems unlikely he considered that.

Albert certainly did not have the anti-social record Ted had but he was not one to worry about others. He went from job to job as it pleased him and he probably joined the service because he knew he would eventually be drafted. His impulse control was a little better than Ted's because he was able to communicate his suicidal thoughts to his family the night before he died despite the fact the signals were unheeded directly. In view of this, that Albert's family was somewhat more supportive to him than Ted's, it is interesting that Albert made some "cry for help" although it was a rather belated one. It would seem to indicate that he felt his family had not totally abandoned him. Still, like most families, they didn't know what to do and were unable to avert Albert's suicide.

Ted did not give many clues except perhaps his silence when he was unable to find his wife. In retrospect, his apparent joy at learning she would take him back certainly was a clue to his deep feelings and need for her. Still, no one picked up his severe disappointment at not finding her as a clue to his suicide. One by one his family left him in order to go to bed. When he was finally alone, he killed himself. His family was completely surprised since Ted presented the outward signs of a "happy, jolly person." He internalized his stressful feelings and this is probably the utmost explanation for his suicide. When it came to deep, personalized emotions, Ted only knew how to "take them out on himself." Petty crimes were only an outlet for some of his other internalized minor feelings. In any event, nothing seemed to compensate for major losses.

At best, one can only pose certain plausible explanations for the suicides of these men; there are no apparent "hard and fast" reasons why they saw fit to end their lives. Impulsivity, family psychological and financial impoverishment, a large family, an uncaring attitude on the part of the family, and the inability to accept help even when offered are some of the major features common to the life style of each of these men. Taken together, they only offer a few possibilities. From these two persons' life histories, the ultimate cause of impulsive suicide remains unknown at present.

3

THE PLANNED SUICIDE

PSYCHOLOGICAL AUTOPSY ON
JANET FREDERICK

J ANET FREDERICK WAS born in New England fifty-one years ago. She was the third of five siblings, having an older sister and brother, and two younger sisters. These siblings grew up in what was described as a stable home situation, living in a family residence which was headed by a dominant father. All the children attended the local schools.

Janet was different from her siblings; she was the introvert of the family; she was also her father's favorite. She was very quiet, yet very stubborn; one sister described her as a person who would "cut off her nose to spite her face." She was also a proud person. For example, during high school when she learned that a boy she had dated steadily and with whom she was in love was dating another girl, she proudly refused to see him ever again. As she was growing up she was always unusually quiet, read a great deal, and was very neat and orderly. She retained this trait for meticulousness throughout her life.

When Janet graduated from high school she entered a school of nursing. Within two weeks she called her father, desperate with homesickness; she immediately returned home. A short while later she became employed by the telephone company where she worked for approximately twenty years. Her brother and sisters eventually married and moved out of the family home into their own homes within the community. Janet remained with her parents.

Her siblings handled stress by blowing up and letting off "steam"; Janet withdrew. She did not expect a great deal from others towards her but it is clear she expected a lot from herself. She was orderly, compulsive, and did not want to make any mistakes. Often she would look as though she were ready to cry because of her sad expression but she didn't cry openly very often.

It was obvious that her major methods of handling stress were withdrawal and retreat. What she did share, she shared with one sister but even then it was always sketched lightly so that no one really knew how Janet felt. When faced with an upsetting episode, she would stay at home and become more quiet. She never used alcoholic beverages.

When she was thirty she asked a sister if she could come and live with her and her family. At the same time this new living arrangement was instituted, she asked the telephone company to put her on the night shift because, as she later explained to her sister, "It might help." At this time she had developed colitis and was upset but she wouldn't reveal her problems to anyone. She sat around her sister's home acting lazy; the sister felt she was depressed. Not long after this she resigned from her position at the telephone company but continued to live with her sister for another two to three years. At this point, she then returned to live with her parents.

In December 1953 she became employed as an accountant-clerk for a large local business. A sister recalled that Janet was angry at this time but no one could discover the cause. Janet would say, "Nobody understands," but then wouldn't express her feelings to anyone. She stayed with this job a few years and then quit. A short time later she gained employment as a secretary with another local business. In the meantime her father had died of lung cancer.

Three years later she changed her job again. The sister with whom she had lived a few years before also worked in this office but only on a part-time basis. Janet had one of her closest relationships with this sister but as they worked together they rarely talked. Janet infrequently initiated conversation and her sister, aware of her sensitivity and feelings of inferiority, didn't seek her out. After two years Janet was tearful and nervous on the job and she quit impulsively. Her co-workers and supervisor were pleased with her and her work; it was Janet who didn't feel comfortable in the job. She felt she was slowing down on the job. At this time she went to a psychiatrist in a nearby city for a few sessions. She broke off this contact. On Thanksgiving she entered a state hospital for the first time saying to her sister, "I've pushed myself as far as I can. All doctors and pills—I can't go on." Her mother had died from complications arising from diabetes just two months before this hospitalization.

During hospitalization she improved and after her release she was treated by one of the hospital's out-patient clinics. Sometimes during this period she would call her sister from her inherited parents' home where she now resided. She would ask her to come and sit with her because she was lonely. These calls, frequently at 10:00 P.M. or later at night, would contain the statement, "I don't want to be alone."

The following summer Janet was employed again as a legal secretary. As usual her work was reported to be satisfactory and she was liked by her employer. She continued to remain in the inherited home and lived there alone for the last two years of her life when she was not in the state hospital.

As would be suspected, Janet was a very unobtrusive, remarkably quiet and reticent person. This was evidenced throughout her life and was shown further in the fact that within her residence at the hospital, according to the staff, she "blended right into the woodwork." At the hospital her affect was described as grossly blunted; it was as if she didn't get touched by many parts of life, as if she didn't feel the same things other people felt. It was also clear that, when she felt life, she gave only mild expression to that feeling if she gave any expression at all.

In the meantime she remained in the hospital making frequent visits to her home and family members. While on visits she became a good friend of a retired sixty-two year old man, a long-time neighbor of Janet's and her family; he was never considered a boyfriend. He was an attractive man with strong ego functioning expressed in a directness towards life. During Janet's last winter he suggested that they attend a skating event at the local arena. Janet accepted, which surprised him, for to his knowledge, this was the first time she had ever sought entertainment where there was a crowd. But they went and Janet seemed to enjoy herself very much.

Each Spring Janet talked about and worked in her garden. In the Spring of 1968 she didn't show any interest in it at all. This was a few months before her death.

Twelve days prior to her death her neighbor male friend picked her up at the hospital and brought her to her home. On this particular morning she seemed somewhat excited because she had a new job at the hospital's vocational rehabilitation center for which she would be paid. She had helped in some of the offices on a part-time basis and now she was going to be working full-time. She was very pleased to be returning to work full-time. The confident sister had encouraged her in her new position. The job wasn't beyond her capabilities and she reassured Janet that the family would stand by her to help her in any way they could when she was released from the hospital.

On her last Sunday alive she went to church with her neighbor friend and his family and returned to his home for breakfast. Then she and her friend, plus his dog, drove to his summer cottage at a nearby lake. That day when he returned from a walk in the rain with his dog, she laughed when the dog ran to her and shook himself dry. He reported that during this day she seemed very calm and relaxed. The day went well but the neighbor never saw her again.

Janet had a paucity of relationships outside her immediate family. Her retired friend was a casual and interested friend. But he let her go her way and he definitely went his. He offered her no pity and never asked her how things were going. Her contacts with patients and staff within the hospital were guarded.

It might be conjectured that her sense of well-being and sense of feeling worthwhile were directly related to her ability to work and be productive as an employee. As her work experiences became shorter and less satisfactory, her life became increasingly unsettled.

While she had many casual acquaintances in the town through her family, her school days, and her employments and these all thought well of her, her closest personal relationship seemed to be limited to one sister. Janet was a person who could not take or accept life on a day-to-day basis as her sister often encouraged her to do; she always had to look ahead and plan. Janet always expressed a great many reservations about her possible failure on her new job. Her sister said that Janet felt if she failed at this job in vocational rehabilitation that it would be the last straw, and she would have to remain in the hospital permanently. Janet had further told many of the patients that she was going to be released for good in two weeks, a plan which was unknown to the staff of the hospital.

Despite her discouragement over what she felt to be unsatisfactory performance on her job, Janet had two specific dates to keep and one trip planned at the time of her death. On the day of her death, a Thursday, she was to have made sandwiches for the hospital canteen with a girl in the rehabilitation center. She reminded this girl a few times of their joint obligation; the patient later told personnel that it was as if Janet were telling her to be sure to do it because "she wouldn't be there." Janet also had planned to babysit for her sister on the forthcoming Saturday night. In addition, she and her male neighbor had planned to go to Boston to tour in the near future.

It was noticed that her nervousness increased when she started working for pay and working full-time. At this time she was receiving an antidepressant medication. Two days before her death she had a long sleepless night. What caused the difficulty was never determined but she woke up frequently and had trouble getting back to sleep. The next day a nurse and social worker noticed that Janet looked wan and pale. She appeared emaciated and there was a gray color to her complexion like that of a cancerous patient. She was given a physical examination that day which did not reveal any physical illnesses.

With a sedative medication she had a good night's sleep. The following morning she signed herself out of the hospital after breakfast. Her first check covering the work on her new job was due the following day.

Before leaving the hospital that morning, personnel had observed and noted that she seemed much better. The paleness which was so apparent the previous day was gone from her face. She had slept very well the previous night; she seemed more relaxed and had a smile on her face. When she approached the ward nurse and said, "I'd like to take the day off and walk in the sun," the request was not so unusual for chronic patients as to be denied. This extremely shy, withdrawn woman smiled and seemed almost outgoing as she signed herself out of the hospital for the morning.

She walked directly downtown to a local sports shop. There she purchased a .32 caliber snub-nosed revolver and a box of fifty .32 caliber cartridges. She volunteered the information to the salesman that she lived alone and wanted the weapon for protection. When she filled out the registration form for the handgun and signed the affidavits, the salesman noticed her name and remarked that he used to know her father. The two talked for awhile and she left the store at mid-morning. Throughout this transaction and conversation, she appeared very "normal" to the salesman. She was neither in a hurry nor did she seem at all anxious. There was nothing about her countenance or demeanor that was unusual. She appeared relaxed, calm and smiled appropriately during this time in the store.

When an afternoon patient-personnel meeting was held at the hospital in the vocational rehabilitation center, Janet was missed. She was to have returned by this time. Two vocational rehabilitation employees became concerned and alarmed and tried to telephone her at her home in the city. When there was no response, they for some reason decided to go to her residence. Through the windows they could see her lying on the floor. Immediately they contacted the hospital security officers and the local city police were notified.

A few minutes later a group of these people entered Janet's home through an unlocked back door. Janet was found lying on her back on the floor of the dining room. Her hands were cold and the blood on her face had dried. There was a .32 caliber revolver on the floor adjacent to her waist on the right side. She had died from a gunshot through the roof of her mouth. She was fully clothed, wearing a blouse, light green skirt, nylon hose, and black shoes.

The neighbor male friend said, "You could have knocked me

over with a feather. I never would have believed it." Patients at the hospital were shocked but consoled themselves by saying, "Janet was nervous—that's the way she was." Some denied it; others became harbingers of bad news. Her brother couldn't believe it and her sister didn't think Janet would ever commit suicide.

Miss Frederick clearly intended to take her own life. One gets the distinct impression as the personality of Janet Frederick unfolds that regardless of whatever suicide prevention services might be established, they wouldn't have picked her up—she would have slipped through the net, however well-trained the professionals might have been.

One can speculate on why she killed herself even though in life she was a remote person and in death, she was even more elusive. Firstly, she built a trap for herself. On the one hand she told other patients she was going to be relased within two weeks permanently—this was not based on fact. Secondly, her job experiences grew shorter and shorter and less satisfactory. She felt she wasn't satisfactory on her new job and failure in it meant permanent hospitalization. How could she cut off her nose to spite her face?

JANET FREDERICK

Janet Frederick was a "model patient" in a psychiatric hospital. She had few wants and few demands. She made little trouble for anyone. In fact, this was her life style except for herself. She was a very dependent person but never to the point of being obnoxious. Her employment history was stable but stormy and in recent years uncertain. She held responsible positions. Underneath all of this lay a great deal of insecurity. Fortunately, she recognized her need for psychiatric help and entered private treatment. But, unfortunately, she did not continue with this treatment and chose to enter a hospital where she would get less personal attention. This may be regarded as the "beginning of the end" for her since her dependency needs were probably fostered even more than that with a favored sister.

She withdrew and became still more socially isolated. Her one interest was in gardening, a "loner's" avocation; the unfortunate loss of this interest prior to her suicide was one more link in the chain that led her to suicide. Even with her family's and gentleman friend's support, she was still unable to gain her self-confidence.

Her "nervousness" increased when she was working full-time for pay. One wonders if she felt herself worthy of this situation and possibly faced another employment failure.

As the psychological autopsy indicates, she had this job while still in the hospital. Her physical condition was excellent; but the important aspects of this fatality were the subtle secretive signals which went unrecognized by hospital staff and others.

Janet's choice of the technique of suicide was unusual for a female and may be an indicator of the strong feelings of hostility that she probably had. She chose a way of death more commonly used by men.

Janet certainly did not give many clearly detectable clues but only a few indications of a "well planned" impending suicide. She had slept well the night before, was noted to be relaxed with a smile on her face when she left the hospital the morning she killed herself "to take a walk in the sun."

PSYCHOLOGICAL AUTOPSY ON
SARAH CANTEL

SARAH CANTEL WAS born in a medium-sized Massachusetts city in the mid-thirties. She spent her first fourteen years there with her family.

At the age of fourteen, she and her younger sister moved to New Hampshire with their parents. As far as could be determined her life through the eleventh grade was without major medical problems or complications. Among her friends she was known as a "wild girl."

She knew that her father's first wife killed herself with stove gas in the thirties. This woman was described as being very depressed and, although this occurred before Sarah's birth, she was aware of the event and the circumstances. In addition, another suicide occurred in the family when an uncle shot himself while in England during World War II. The details of this were not known to the family but Sarah was aware of this suicide and discussed it with her mother and her husband. She did not dwell on this death until she brought it up again to her mother within two years of her own suicide.

At the midterm of her senior year in high school, Sarah informed her parents that she was pregnant. This unfortunate incident forced her to miss the last part of her senior year and graduation although she received her high school diploma at a later date. She kept her child and when the baby was 1½ years old, she went with Sarah into her marriage.

Mrs. Cantel fell midway between being a very neat and orderly person and a disorderly person. This was true in her formative years as well as after her marriage. As a girl she was carefree and obedient—perhaps too obedient according to her mother. She was outgoing and possessed a marvelous sense of humor. She was very well-liked by all the neighbors. She was described as a person in love with life, with a zest for it, and one who had a great spirit.

Mrs. Cantel moved from being a very carefree youth to a very responsible adult. She was very concerned and attentive to her children. At her death there were four children: two girls, aged thirteen and seven, and two boys, aged ten and one. She was able to assume a healthy maternal role in the family despite her feelings of inadequacy and her periods of hospitalization. About two years before her suicide, she had been hospitalized a total of five times. Her husband reported that life didn't seem to get her down, that she was able to take disappointments in her stride.

In her final years of high school and before she married, Sarah reportedly drank heavily. No one knew exactly how heavily but she told her husband and her mother that she was an alcoholic during this period. After her marriage her alcoholic intake dwindled until it was mild to moderate; it was always well controlled until a few months before her death. At that time she resumed drinking heavily according to her husband. She had an insatiable appetite for alcohol, he claimed, and he could not keep enough to drink in the house. She would go through a six-pack of beer very quickly, consuming the contents of more than two six-packs at one sitting and demanded more. At last her husband refused to buy any more toward the final month of her life. She didn't seem to care whether she had anything to drink or not and didn't ask him for any alcohol.

Sarah's father died about nine months before her own death. With his death it appears she lost the one person she was especially close to, and the result of this loss was greatly upsetting to her. Formerly a frequent visitor to her parents' home, it was nearly a month and a half following her father's death that she could go there. But even this great loss, as upsetting as it was to her, was rarely mentioned by Mrs. Cantel to other members of the family.

One prevailing thought stayed in Mrs. Cantel's mind but she shared it only with her minister friend and never to any family members. She was torn by the thought and belief that she had killed her father by simply failing to do anything to prevent his death. The depth of feeling and communication between her and her father seems to stand out as unique in Mrs. Cantel's life. For example, her father had rid the house of his extensive gun collection with one exception. He disarmed that weapon and when Mrs. Cantel found it, he said, "That won't do you much good, Sarah." Just prior to his death he predicted to the chief of police that Sarah would take her own life.

Sarah's first request to be buried in the small exclusive family cemetery was made to her mother two years prior to Mrs. Cantel's death. This question was answered positively and all succeeding answers to this same question posed by Mrs. Cantel were positive but, on this first occasion, her mother noted her daughter felt life was slipping away. This request, almost a plea, for reassurance was asked again any number of times with the final time being on the morning of her death. Mrs. Cantel's mother was driving her home when the question came, "Will you promise me one thing—that I may be buried in the little family cemetery?" Her mother again reassured her.

Sarah was a steady woman according to informants. She did not show any signs of being upset to others but inside she was tormented. Even her husband was not aware of this. However, he supported her when she made two visits to a local psychiatrist. In the fall of the same year she again sought psychiatric help from the local community mental health center. She was so upset and depressed during that visit, the clinic recommended voluntary hospitalization. The following day Mrs. Cantel voluntarily committed herself to a mental hospital for the first of a series of hospitalizations.

Her dominant feeling was that she had to get away from herself. With a calm and unruffled exterior which fooled her husband and other family members, she was constantly tormented within. "I'm no good because I've had an illegitimate child and I drank a good deal when I was younger." She often discussed suicide with her minister friend. He was not her minister but had befriended her upon her hospitalization. He stated that she did not discuss suicide dispassionately but with a good deal of feeling.

During the last six months of her life, her feelings of guilt about her oldest daughter and the death of her father increased. She kept these feelings to herself and only rarely did she share them with her mother, husband, or, in the case of her father's death, the minister.

At the same time she became preoccupied with her tongue. From time to time it would break out with small sores. Her husband and her doctor concluded it was "nerves" but a specialist gave her some medication which reduced the condition. While the sores diminished and greatly subsided, her preoccupation with her tongue increased. She was convinced that she looked terrible. In the month of her death, she went to a medical center in order to determine whether her condition was cancerous or not. She had already arrived at this conclusion as part of her preoccupation. However, the facts did not support her concern and she was so informed. Her husband came to measure the degree to which she was depressed by the time she spent looking at and inspecting her tongue. It looked quite normal to him aside from the small scar tissue. Yet the first thing every morning she would inspect it usually with a hand mirror while lying on the bed. These inspections occurred throughout the day with some lasting just a few minutes, others between five and ten minutes. This preoccupation remained until she died and she was never convinced that her tongue was not cancerous.

The Cantels reportedly had a satisfactory marital life. Mr. Cantel always supported her during her emotional upsets. Their sexual relationship was also gratifying for both of them. But on two occasions Mrs. Cantel moved outside her marriage to have intercourse. The first occasion happened just a few days prior to her father's death when she intended to go to the hospital for the day but instead went to Boston by bus. After spending the night with a man, she had a woman call her husband to come and get her, which he did. He felt she did this to hurt him but Sarah didn't know why she would want to hurt him.

The second occasion occurred at the time of her discharge

from the hospital. She announced to her husband that she again had spent a night with a man.

Only on very rare occasions would Mrs. Cantel shout or throw something at her husband or the children. By far her most frequent reaction to stress was withdrawal, silence, and an outward stance of passivity and acquiesence. The denial of feelings was marked and her mother and husband both said that Mrs. Cantel was exceedingly adroit about completely covering her feelings.

In September 1966 her husband and the children discovered the body of a neighbor woman who had committed suicide with an overdose of sleeping pills very close to the family home. Sarah was close by but did not view the scene. The uncle, behind whose home the body was found, said it upset Sarah greatly. Her husband reported that after a few days she rarely mentioned the event. She did express great feelings for the loss that must have been suffered by the surviving husband.

Mrs. Cantel never felt she was useful to her own family. Aside from her previous suicide attempts and her series of hospitalizations, it seemed clear she was not much better during the last six weeks before her death than at any previous time in the last two years. She had said to her sister a year ago that if anything happened to her she would not worry because the family could take care of themselves. Shortly before her death she told her husband that her death was planned, including the method, but when her husband pressed for details, she refused to elaborate. Following her first suicide attempt, she told her husband three or four times that if he had a gun she would have shot herself. He had a gun but she did not know it. Sarah never came right out and told her husband she was planning to commit suicide but she would often say to him that she didn't have any desire to go on living.

Her first suicide attempt occurred in late winter of the year prior to her death. She called her husband while he was at work and told him she was going to kill herself. Then she slashed her wrists with a razor. She chose a time within ten minutes of the hour when her children normally returned from school. As a result of this episode and on the recommendation of her family doctor, she voluntarily admitted herself to the mental hospital.

Her second attempt occurred the following summer. Her husband had stopped off at his mother's house while returning from work. The telephone rang and when his mother answered it there was no response from the caller. The mother remarked that this had happened just before he arrived. The telephone rang again with the same results. The fourth time it rang Mr. Cantel answered and his wife said, "I've done it." He asked, "You've done what?" She said, "I've taken an overdose." He called the emergency police rescue squad; she was taken to the hospital to have her stomach pumped and then transferred to the mental hospital the same day.

Her last period of hospitalization began that fall and terminated about a month prior to her death. She had home privileges for a day's visit before the Thanksgiving holiday. Her husband found her in the bedroom trying to kill herself. She had taken the cord off his bathrobe and attempted to hang herself from a bedpost. Her husband again found her in time.

Two days before her death, her husband noted her to be a little depressed but he felt she was better than on most mornings. On Sunday the family planned to go to Sarah's mother's house. When she awoke Sunday morning she was very depressed and didn't want to follow the intended plans. The family shifted their plans accordingly; but by noon she had changed her mind and they went to her mother's home. As it happened, Sarah almost boldly walked into the house with her family coming behind. She put her arms around her mother and asked, "Can I stay overnight?" Her mother agreed since this was a request which had been made before. Sarah informed her husband of the plan; he accepted it without question. They all reminded each other that she had an appointment with her psychiatrist at the mental hospital the following day.

The family spent the afternoon fixing up the family cemetery. The grass was cut and trimming was done. Sarah and her youngest child only stayed about a half hour, with Sarah saying she wasn't feeling well and was going to return to the house.

Later in the afternoon for some reason she returned to the cemetery for a brief time.

Her husband and children returned home late Sunday afternoon and she and her mother went to pick up a friend for dinner. This was pleasurable for the threesome and later in the evening the friend was returned home. On the drive back to her mother's home, Sarah remarked that she felt chilled and couldn't get warm. She mentioned this two or three times during the drive. Her mother helped her to bed and got her a hot water bottle. She slept well Sunday night.

The following morning she called her husband to see if the children were getting off to school and that all was well. Later her mother drove her home after her husband had gone to work. Earlier, the couple had arranged that Mr. Cantel would come home after lunch; Sarah would drive him back to work and then would take the car for her appointment with her psychiatrist at the hospital. This part of the day went according to plan and Mr. Cantel recalled that his wife was very calm and serene. She even remarked, "What a nice day it is" and when he told her that his new business was doing better this month, she seemingly was pleased. While she was often a little more talkative before therapy sessions, this day she seemed more talkative than usual.

When she dropped her husband off at his employment, it was the last time she was seen alive. Later when she did not pick up her husband at work, he became concerned. An hour later he called Sarah's mother who, although she tried to allay his fears, had felt all day at her place of employment that she would not be at work the following day.

For some reason, while a friend was visiting the mother about an hour later, she noticed that the vacuum cleaner in the corner of the kitchen didn't have the hose with it. She became worried and called her son-in-law. He immediately became concerned and instructed Sarah's mother to have the uncle who lived next door go to the family park about three hundred yards behind her house to see if Mrs. Cantel was there. The uncle walked to the family glen and park, the private family burial place. As he did so, Sarah's mother drove across the field behind her house towards the same place. She spotted the roof of her daughter's car and immediately summoned the police and medical examiner.

Sarah, fully clothed, was lying across the front seat of the car. The ignition was on, the motor running, and the radio was playing softly. All windows of the car were closed except the right rear one which was open just enough to fit the vacuum cleaner hose through the opening with a stuffed towel. The other end of the hose was attached to the exhaust pipe.

During the last six months of her life, Sarah said occasionally to her mother, "I'm afraid." When her mother asked her why, she said, "I don't know why, I'm just afraid and no one seems to understand me." Her mother couldn't understand why a person who formerly loved to be alone and sought solitude now was a person afraid to be alone. She seemed to have no fear of death or accidents yet she did have a fear of having cancer of the tongue.

There were a few changes, aside from her illness, noted in her life during the last two years. Her sleeping habits seemed to have remained relatively constant. Her appetite improved in the last six weeks over any previous period in the preceding two years, a somewhat strange pattern in suicidal persons. However, her interest in cooking diminished.

The minister who befriended her felt they had a particularly close relationship; they seemed to be "on the same wave-length." They could communicate easily and well and discussed suicide and death freely. Sarah, on the other hand, never initiated their meetings; he would contact her at the hospital. Sarah felt she was a much worse person than she actually was, according to the respondents. She believed she wasn't good for her family and that she was a useless person. Her self-esteem always seemed low. The image in which others saw her was contradictory to her own self-image. Her husband felt this was one of her major problems.

During the last month she was much more outgoing and one Sunday she attended a concert. She enjoyed this event and the day before her death reiterated how much she had liked it. The last days of her life she was noticeably better, according to both her mother and husband, than they had noted in years.

Sarah Cantel's death was absolutely intentional. She drove to her mother's home and took the vacuum cleaner hose. Then she drove to the family sanctuary. She took the hose and attached it to her car's exhaust pipe. Then she led the hose into the rear window of the car, stuffed the opening with a towel, and lay down to die. Had anyone in the family seen her drive down into the glen they would have thought nothing of it. This was a place she loved and knew well.

She went home to die.

SARAH CANTEL

Sarah Cantel was a somewhat strong-willed woman who constantly suffered with her life problems. She had a long history of doing as she pleased though she was a willing housewife and mother. This was reflected by her multiple contacts with mental health workers and hospitalizations. She had a cancerophobia. She kept a majority of her feelings to herself and did not "broadcast" them. Certainly during the last two years of her life she was probably psychotic; there were probably other episodes earlier which she seemed able to cope with. She continued to develop and enlarge a very poor self-image.

For some reason she became a promiscuous individual, but still her husband loved her, upon whom she showed deep dependency. She presented the perplexing picture of a strong will coupled with passive dependency. All of these crosscurrents were the precipitating factors in Mrs. Cantel's suicide and seemingly resulted in a well-planned self-demise not totally unnoticed by her close family members.

The Planned Suicide

Some suicides can appear to be an impulsive act or an act that "just happened" without a history of careful, conscious, conniving planning. When the latter "type" occurs it contains

some important information which is germane to the study of
suicidology.

Miss Frederick and Mrs. Cantel are good examples of individuals who appear to have given careful planning to their
own demise. Miss Frederick was a patient at the mental hospital
while Mrs. Cantel had been a patient at the same hospital
several times. Each had a history of a serious mental disorder;
both had psychotic diagnoses. Each appeared to have come
through the worst of their illnesses; Miss Frederick was still
hospitalized but working in a vocational rehabilitation program
at the hospital while Mrs. Cantel was out of the hospital and
at home. There were some significant differences; Miss Frederick
was externally a passive, "well-behaved" person; Mrs. Cantel
had a promiscuous youth; she did quiet down as she grew older
but signs of her emotional immaturity were obvious. Sarah had a
problem with alcohol which was not shared by Janet. In addition,
Sarah was beset with cancerophobia, something which was
foreign to Janet.

There are some important similarities shared by these two
women. Both were dependent persons. To what extent this was
fostered by their hospitalizations cannot be assessed. It seems
likely that their dependency needs might likely have been
magnified by the very nature of being hospitalized in a good-
sized mental hospital. Most mental hospitals of this type do not
render much individual personal attention and consequently
resort to doing many everyday things for its patients, thus
obviating the underlying dependency.

Miss Frederick gave only a minimum amount of clues to her
suicide. It is felt that the clues were there; notably the authors
wonder what her remark about going for a "walk in the sun"
actually meant. There has to be a psychological implication.
Her life was really planned, consciously or unconsciously, which
ultimately led up to her suicide. In retrospect, knowing her
life history, it would seem that she were predestined to take
her own life.

Sarah's plans very obviously were more transparent. As a
youth she went through a somewhat wild and promiscuous

period as evidenced by her drinking and illegitimate child. She talked of plans for her burial which is unusual for someone as young as she. Further, shortly before her death she told her husband that her death was planned—even down to indicating the method. She had attempted suicide three times prior to the completed act. Her final act of suicide was carefully planned so as not to be detected before her death, although both her husband and her mother were suspicious. One can see, even from these two unfortunate persons, that the planned suicide is hard to judge, even in retrospect. A particular kind of compulsive personality type tends to become involved in this type of suicide. The compulsive element seems to take over in the methodical planning. In both of these examples a psychotic component provides sufficient insulation from reality to allow the act to take place.

The planned suicide is a blend of the conscious and unconscious such that it is almost impossible for one to differentiate one from the other. One can see varying degrees of planning in both of these two cases. Janet probably made fewer plans than did Sarah but her intentions were just as deadly. Sarah was probably the sicker of the two but she was still able to carry her plan to completion. The perception of suicide as a "way out" dawned gradually on each of these women and, as it did, each one turned to what seemed to be her inevitable fate.

4

THE MINIMUM SIGNAL SUICIDE

PSYCHOLOGICAL AUTOPSY ON
ARTHUR PALMER

ARTHUR PALMER WAS the youngest of three siblings. His brother, four years his senior, lived in a nearby state as did his sister who was two years older than he. Both siblings were married. Arthur's father died five years before his death of a stomach disorder. He had several hospitalizations for internal bleeding. Either ulcers or cancer was suspected. His mother was in good health and retired. This family was described as being very "close." They kept in touch with one another by telephone and visited each other quite frequently.

Mr. Palmer grew up and went to school in southern New England. He was always popular and well-liked. His academic achievement was average. He met his wife in the eighth grade and they dated throughout high school. He graduated from high school at the age of seventeen and enlisted into the armed services during World War II. He and his girl friend corresponded regularly during this time. He re-enlisted in his early twenties although his teenage future wife did not approve.

They finally married when he was twenty-six years old. Following the marriage Arthur remained with the military until 1961, having been stationed in Europe, the Southwest, and finally at a New England base for the last eleven years of his enlistment. At this time he retired and worked as a civilian in the same military station in the accounting division.

Arthur always aspired to being a businessman and finally sought legal counsel for this in 1965. He had worked and saved money and finally borrowed several thousand dollars from his mother to open a restaurant in 1968. This was much against his wife's wishes. She was a very dependent, insecure person who worried about the money involved. On the one hand she said he "could do anything," but with ambivalence felt that he could not do it. She opposed him all the way in this new venture and only with a great apprehension finally allowed herself at least to go along with the enterprise. She even went to the point of becoming responsible for transporting funds from the restaurant to the bank, etc.

Mrs. Palmer described herself as a person who had always been highly nervous and prone to depression. The year of her husband's death, she sought psychiatric help at a mental health clinic where she was evaluated as a basically dependent personality with chronic anxiety and depression. She was placed on medication and was seen for five visits. The couple was seen on one occasion conjointly at the request of the examining doctor. Arthur was found to be a jovial, capable man, reassuring, supportive, and somewhat fatherly toward his wife. Following her husband's death she admitted that if anyone in the family were to think of someone's committing suicide, it would have been she rather than her husband.

Mr. Palmer was in excellent health. He was geared towards productivity in life and worked twelve to eighteen hours a day to open the restaurant. This all began in the spring of 1968. He personally purchased equipment which he helped to install, fixed floors, tables, hired a staff of about a dozen to handle the mechanics of producing meals. He was meticulous and thorough in his work and an able and a respected organizer. He did lose twelve pounds during the first two weeks of the restaurant's opening but amazed his physician with his excellent blood pressure during a routine medical examination.

Michael was the Palmer's only child. He was a good-looking, clean-cut youth who, just having graduated from high school, had been accepted at the university for the fall term. In high school Mike played baseball, was on the student council, was a member of the National Honor Society, and was the president of the Spanish Club. Both of his parents attended school events regularly and took an active participation in Mike's interests.

Mr. Palmer was a devoted father and perhaps a doting husband; he was also a source of strength to his son whom he adored and took great pride. He intended to prepare and educate his son in business matters. In this respect he was compulsive and a self-driven accomplisher directed toward establishing goals.

Arthur was also known for his reliability and conscientiousness with anything he undertook. He was outgoing, got along very well with everyone, and was a respected member of the community. Words most often used to describe him were "cheerful, easy-going, quiet, and down-to-earth, likeable." He was a capable person who never spoke of problems and confided in no one about his personal affairs. His wife had only a vague understanding of his business venture in spite of "cooperating." He always attempted to protect her from worry. He humored people, was seldom angered, and never lost his temper. With his son, he was an available listener and sometimes offered guidance. He never ordered anyone to do anything but rather asked and suggested. He involved his son in the business thinking that it was a good learning experience for Mike. He was very predictable, always being on time and he would telephone if he was going to be delayed. He often asked what he could do for others, especially his wife. He was described as one who "always took care of everything." He did not smoke or drink. He ate and slept well until about a month prior to his death. Mr. Palmer was a confident man who had tremendous ideas of financial success but no experience in self-employment. At the age of forty-eight when he retired from the armed services, it was his first completely independent step to prove himself. He was acutely aware of others' dependence on him, a role which he assumed seemingly with comfort. Consciously, he did not recognize or accept his own dependence. He had always provided consistently, carefully, and well for his family. This adaptation was seriously threatened in his mind at the time of death and he had experienced guilt for involving his family in his restaurant business. He was very worried about the success or failure of his business because of the amount of his mother's money he had borrowed and invested. He reacted by working harder and by putting in many hours physically and pouring over the financial business sheets. He became a more frequent caller at his attorney's which seemed an appropriate action for someone whose business was just getting underway.

Although there were repeated assurances from a reliable advisor, Mr. Palmer felt his business was failing. He could not be convinced that losses were to be expected the first month of the operation; the balance sheet showed losses for the two weeks of the operation that Mr. Palmer lived (the business is now thriving). He became more and more preoccupied with how much he had borrowed to make the investment and worried that he had made a mistake. His keen sense of responsibility became his avenger.

From the last week in June to his death three weeks later, he worked himself to exhaustion. He sometimes worked as many as twenty hours a day. A couple of nights before his death, he was so tired that he did not undress for bed; he just lay down beside his wife. The night before he died, the whole family went to bed at the same hour, about 1:00 A.M. when he came in from work. He did not brush his teeth and commented that he was so tired he almost didn't come in from the car. He and his wife had not had sexual relations for several weeks and he was too tired to even kiss her good night as he usually did.

Mr. Palmer's attorney was the only one in whom Mr. Palmer confided; it was assumed his anxiety was mounting daily as he increased his contact with the attorney. Mr. Palmer's state of physical exhaustion was apparent to all; however, his personality pattern did not change markedly. In the last few days before his death he could not grasp the logic and figures as clearly or rapidly. In his mind that meant things were going poorly in his business. He also became more concerned about his wife's failure to be of support. Her manner was one of grim acceptance with repeated questions and voicings of her lack of faith in the venture. He gave his son days off "when he could" but took none himself. Mrs. Palmer's mother was dying of cancer, an added burden to her and whom she faithfully visited once a week. This was where she was the day Mr. Palmer killed himself, and this illness in the family must have been an added strain on her and, subsequently, on him since Mrs. Palmer leaned so heavily on her husband.

There was no evidence that Mr. Palmer manifested any

premonitions, fears, thoughts, fantasies, or dreams with reference to death. He certainly feared failure in business but had no known fears of any other nature.

On the day of her husband's death, Mrs. Palmer made lunch for him as he usually came home for lunch. Then she went to the restaurant to pick up the previous day's receipts to take them to the bank. She recalled nothing unusual about her husband, took the money to the bank, and left for daily Mass around 11:00 A.M. Mike also left before lunch to go swimming at the pool of a friend with whom he went golfing in the afternoon. It was his first day off from work at the restaurant in twelve days.

Mike arrived home in the late afternoon. The door of the single-car garage, which was attached to the house, was closed and Mike heard the motor of a car running. He opened the garage door, saw his father in the car with a length of vacuum hose in his mouth. He pulled the hose out of his mouth and then removed his father from the car. Mr. Palmer was not breathing and the son called an ambulance. Mr. Palmer was pronounced dead on arrival at the hospital at 6:15 P.M. After examination, the medical referee reported death "due to carbon monoxide poisoning."

Mr. Palmer's death was intentional. He was assured of time, knowing his family would be otherwise occupied for a definite period of time. The only variables were the son's possibly returning home or a neighbor's intervention. The latter was unlikely since that time of day was business hours for his neighbor. Mr. Palmer was as "matter of fact" and concise about his death as he was about his life.

ARTHUR PALMER

Here is a man whom we have called the "minimum signal suicide." He was meticulous, compulsive, and well-liked by everyone. He borrowed money to go into business for himself. At first he did not do as well as he had expected. He was working twenty hours a day, falling into bed with his clothes on. He had not expressed discouragement or depression to anyone. It would seem that he simply could not stand what he perceived as an impending failure.

The Minimum Signal Suicide

A great deal has been written about individuals who send out cries for help during a suicidal crisis. Studies have been made about those who suicide while exhibiting a serious physical or mental illness and, in general, there are a number of references dealing with suicide associated with other abnormal conditions.

It is difficult to find much in the literature about people who are functioning within normal limits and give few or no apparent clues to their impending suicide. The description of these individuals, let alone the explanation of why they commit suicide, is seen infrequently.

One author sees the general principle that ". . . the deeper the Depressive Reaction and the more premeditated and planned the attempt, the more obscure will be the communication of suicidal intent."[1] The same author also proposes seven points, each to be rated on a scale of one to seven in increasing order of severity as a tentative means of assessing potential for suicide. The seven points are the following: "(1) Early morning awakening; (2) 'Morning Ebb-Tide of Spirits;' (3) Level of Interests; (4) Initial or sudden improvement; (5) Withdrawal; (6) Communicability; (7) Presence of remorse (after suicidal attempt)."[2]

An application of *this* scale to the details available from the life of Arthur Palmer results in a score in the "critical" range. An overall clinical impression of Mr. Palmer's life, even just prior to his death, does not portray the usual picture of a man about to commit suicide. Mr. Palmer was the prototype of the masculine "pillar of strength" on whom his family, particularly his wife, depended for almost everything.

Although he suffered a recent weight loss, he still remained in excellent health. His whole life-style was one of extreme thoroughness and meticulousness, bordering on compulsivity.

---

1. Laughlin, Henry P.: *The Neuroses.* Appleton, 1967, p. 204.
2. *Ibid.* pp. 163-164.

Still, he was outgoing and well-liked and respected in the community. It is said of him that he "always took care of everything." For many years he was able to do just that. This character trait eventually proved to be his downfall.

The day of his death, Mr. Palmer gave no *apparent* indications of his intended suicide. In retrospect it can be seen that he picked a time when everyone was out and discovery was most unlikely. He picked a highly lethal method, carbon monoxide poisoning in a closed garage. His death certainly was assured. Mr. Palmer's death-style was consistent with his life-style. He was careful, thorough, and meticulous.

What was it that led this man to the fateful decision to take his own life? Mr. Palmer's behavior can be interpreted as conforming with the model of the well-planned and intended suicide as described in this book. But he differed so greatly from the well-planned suicide in that he gave so little in the way of clues to his demise. He was silent and, as far as can be determined, never voiced any ideas about suicide.

One idea to be considered is that he did not know how to "cry for help;" he had always been fiercely independent and self-reliant. He did not understand or could not bring himself to ask for help from appropriate persons such as a friend, relatives, a clergyman, or his family doctor. That aspect of the communication process either had broken down or was not completely developed.

The manner in which one would go about preventing a suicide of this type under ordinary circumstances remains unclear. The clues were so few and so subtle that one would be hard-pressed to detect them while in the process. There is no ready solution to this especially perplexing type of suicide.

5

THE PSYCHOTIC SUICIDE

PSYCHOLOGICAL AUTOPSY ON
JOHN ROGERS

John Rogers was born in a small New England town sixty years ago. He was the youngest of three children, all boys. John entered school when he was six and left at sixteen reportedly because of family difficulties and because he wanted a job. John's parents were divorced when he was very young. The parents lived together for only six years. She divorced her husband because he drank and would not support the family. After the divorce, John never saw his father. The mother re-married when John was nine years old. This marriage lasted about ten years and ended in divorce. There were no children by this second marriage. John reportedly got along with his stepfather until he became a teenager, when his stepfather seemingly became jealous of him. As a result, John left home and school at a relatively young age and became self-supporting.

When he left school he "went West" to see the country. He travelled around by riding freight trains. He worked as an unskilled laborer to earn enough money to keep going. After two years he returned home to live with his mother.

When John was twenty-eight, he married Rhoda Fox. His wife came from the Southwest and they had corresponded for a short time. Each had received the other's name through a "love-lorn" column. This marriage only lasted for about two months because Rhoda became homesick for her family and home. She quickly divorced John and returned home. No children were conceived during this brief time and Mr. Rogers never married again. Little else is known about the marriage. At this time he went back to live with his mother.

John was working for the railroad as a laborer from the age of eighteen until he was twenty-eight. Then he left the railroad for a better-paying job in a manufacturing plant near his mother's home. He remained at this job until he was laid off four years later. He obtained another job as a laborer. He stayed there for one year but became "ill." The nature of this illness was unknown. He then worked for a winter as a mill-hand. This job ended and he began looking for work again. He couldn't find employment and it was at this time his mother first noticed a change in his personality. He was unemployed for five years due to "nervousness" before admission to a mental hospital.

It was noted that John had become easily discouraged and also suspicious. Children in the neighborhood aggravated him and he felt that people were against him. He began to lose his temper quickly and curse. When he walked down the street with his mother and saw a group of people passing by, he would turn to his mother and say, "There goes a bunch of son-of-a-bitches."

He also became grandiose; he felt that he knew more about everything than anyone else. John also developed many somatic complaints and preoccupations and began taking bromides for sleep. Finally, on the advice of his local physician, the mother brought him to the state mental hospital. He was forty-three at this time.

On admission it was noticed that he "felt that everyone is against me and trying to harm me." He was tense, agitated, talked continuously, and showed a flight of ideas. He said, "I'm practically a wreck. I cannot work. My physical health is not good. I have a pain in my abdomen. I am nervous and I can't sleep." He denied any suicidal ideas. During three months of hospitalization, he received four electroshock treatments. After that time, the staff recommendation was that ". . . he can be released as he has shown improvement."

John went home with his mother. During this interval before his readmission, he did not go out, and "made no effort to find a job." He remained at his mother's home for four months and then had to be returned to the hospital. At this time ". . . the patient was excitable, talkative, accused the police officers and the doctor of 'playing a game' with him." For the next four years he remained in the hospital essentially unimproved. With the arrival of tranquilizing medications, John was placed on them and his mental condition improved. He developed extra-pyramidal side effects for this drug and during the next several years received various combinations of tranquilizers and anti-parkinsonian drugs. These were all gradually discontinued but he continued to show "tremor of the hands and, to a lesser degree, tremor of head." A neurological consultation resulted in the diagnostic impression of "Parkinsonism, probably not related to drugs." At this time it was felt that this man was gradually deteriorating both physically and mentally, according to his hospital record:

> In 1967 the patient was described as being "untidy in his personal habits and appearance." He was also "uncooperative and required constant close supervision, care, and attention from the ward personnel. He was also out of contact with his environment and disoriented in all spheres. Physical examination was essentially negative."

Then a year later it was noted that he was:

> "not interested in his personal appearance. Also he was not cooperative. His memory was bad for recent and remote events. He was disoriented. He showed no improvement over the last year. He was on no medication."

For several years John resided on a disturbed ward in the hospital. Most of the patients on this ward were younger than he. Finally in 1968 because of his deterioration, Mr. Rogers was transferred to a geriatric ward. His condition worsened.

At this time a newly-employed physician at the hospital took charge of the building where he resided replacing the physician who had managed this medical service for years.

Two weeks before his death, John was placed on a new anti-depressant medication, hopefully to increase his alertness along with inert psychic and motor activation. The affect of this drug on John was remarkable. Before this medication was prescribed he would not keep his clothes on, would not eat, would not talk to people, and would not come out of his room. Shortly after this new medicine was begun, the psychiatric aides noticed that Mr. Rogers dressed himself, regained his appetite, engaged in conversations, and readily came out of his room frequently. But he also became very agitated. His extra-pyramidal symptoms worsened; he couldn't sit still; he said that the patients where he lived "were all vegetables and goddamn fools," and he asked to be transferred to another ward. This request was denied and a few days later he committed suicide.

On the day of his death, Mr. Rogers had been about the ward. According to two of the psychiatric aides on duty, Mr. Rogers was acting in his usual manner. He was described as seclusive, agitated, and he paced the floor. When the aide brought the patient's supper try to his room where he customarily ate, he found Mr. Rogers hanging from an upended bed by a bedsheet. One end was knotted to the elevated bed legs; the other was around the victim's neck. Artificial respiration was without results. The County Medical Examiner certified the cause of death as asphyxia from hanging.

As far as is known, John gave no clues of his intention to commit suicide; there were no verbal clues and no notes. In retrospect, he did build up toward suicide in a rather classical fashion. Here was an individual emerging from acute depression into an agitated state, accompanied by the physical discomfiture of extra-pyramidal symptoms, wanting and demanding something that was refused, his transfer to another area of the hospital, and having no one whom he trusted to whom he could turn. It would seem that he turned to what he thought was the ultimate escape.

JOHN ROGERS

Mr. Rogers was a man who can best be typed as the psychotic suicide. He was a loner who finally broke down and had to be hospitalized for a total of seventeen years. Shortly before his suicide, he was transferred to a chronic geriatric service in a mental hospital and placed on a medication believed to have alerting properties. This prescription apparently had some effect on him and he asked to be transferred back to his original ward. When this was denied, he committed suicide. It can be speculated "ad infinitum" the reason for this suicide. Probably it was due to the fact that this patient's old surroundings were taken away from him without adequate reassurance and reinforcement in a new environment.

PSYCHOLOGICAL AUTOPSY ON
CONSTANCE KNIGHT

CONSTANCE KNIGHT WAS forty-four years old at the time of her death. She had three siblings, one sister and two brothers. She did not attend school during her early years but, at her mother's insistence, was tutored in the family home. She then attended a private boarding school and finally went on to a well-known women's college where she graduated with a degree in nursing.

Miss Knight, who never married, related that her early life was very unhappy: "I never did anything right and always felt guilty." She recalled being a day-dreamer. She had an imaginary playmate from age five to eight years. Her mother was reported as "being pleased that Constance now has a girl friend."

Constance hated her father; he was known to make everyone miserable and he manipulated the family to get himself attention. In relation to this, she talked a great deal about the odd behavior of her parents and the constant inter-play between them and the obviously emotionally mixed-up siblings. This family seemed to specialize in being non-conventional. The father was a lazy fellow who felt everyone should "wait on him." He prided himself on being an "intellectual," but actually he was an "egocentric ineffectual old man" all his life. The mother lived in another world and actually had minimal contact with her growing children. She enjoyed her friends in the field of art and foreign languages and she functioned as a mother rarely. As it turned out, Constance was raised by her older sisters and a retinue of old housemaids. The family more-or-less thought and spoke of her as the ugly duckling of the family. These inadequate feelings persisted to her death.

Miss Knight found it impossible to express warm genuine feelings for anybody except her brother Bertram who lived alone

74

in New York writing poetry. They were "kindred spirits." Later in life she apparently had a private income that did not make having a job mandatory and it was reported that for a time she slept all day and prowled the streets of a large city alone at night.

Her parents expected her to get the highest grades in everything that she undertook and did not give any preference to what Connie wanted to do in her life. They did this with all their children and as a consequence, all of the children had severe psychiatric problems. Each family member had to live up to being a "Knight." The children, including Constance, were called "stupid and ignorant" in spite of achievements. This compulsivity, enforced by her parents, persisted throughout Connie's life.

Constance also was concerned that she might be homosexual. She never could discuss sex with her mother; she was rebuffed even when she inquired about menstruation. The family reportedly was very peculiar. They dressed the girls as boys and had their hair cut very closely; the boys were dressed in rather effeminate clothes and were not allowed to cut their hair. The boys wore their hair shoulder-length much earlier than the accepted style known in the late Sixties.

The family background was a severe handicap to her in her nursing profession. She was a graduate of a reputable nursing school, but she was working as a visiting home nurse in New York City. She felt that her nursing techniques were poor. This also made it difficult for her to live with herself.

Connie had never been able to allow any warm, personal relationship with anybody and, as a consequence, thought that other people were like her parents who were always critical of her and who thought she was "no good." She recognized that she felt this way about herself and only occasionally was she able to understand that it was a projection of her own feelings to those close to her. In spite of this, she held several nursing jobs, worked in a Settlement House for a number of years where she was efficient and well-liked.

This woman had tremendous dependency needs. She had expressed a desire to die since the late 1940's. When these needs were unmet, she would create a situation or make a request that couldn't be granted. Then she'd sit back and feel mistreated and enjoy her role as an "injustice collector." Constance stated she "wouldn't allow myself to like anyone because they will either expect too much of me or they will turn against me and hurt me." She had made reference to ideas of suicide for twenty-eight years before her death.

Apparently Constance was mentally healthy and able to function until her first illness in 1953 when she vacationed in Europe with relatives. For some reason after her return she was no longer interested in working; she was unable to make decisions. She became very depressed and anxious. She said that she "felt sick" but was not.

She was hospitalized at a private hospital where she had courses of insulin and electroshock treatments with no lasting improvement. She remained there for nine months at which time she was discharged to live with her sister. Constance did not adjust well in this new environment. She deteriorated and began having hallucinations and delusions. After four years she was readmitted to the same private mental hospital. Her family paid for her hospitalization.

At this time her mood was changeable. She was friendly and pleasant but vague, perplexed, and confused. During psychotherapy interviews, she was always the same: profuse verbal productivity, confused, agitated and crying, always asked "When and how can I get out of here?" adding, "Staying is just a waste of time."

In 1959, two months after readmission to this hospital, she started to work in the laundry and adjusted well there. She spent frequent successful visits at home during the next year and she voluntarily asked to be released to home. The family was discouraged by her repeated episodes of psychiatric failure and none of them encouraged her to leave the hospital; none of them requested her release. Her doctor felt that if she could find a job and live in the community, it would be to her benefit. It was his opinion that at least she might gain confidence in herself. Consequently she was given permission to go to an employment agency to find work during the days and staying at the hospital nights. Connie couldn't find a job and became depressed. Later when this depression improved, she said she was glad she couldn't find a job since she felt "I was not well enough," and another failure would have harmed her more.

She repeatedly expressed thoughts of committing suicide. She said she had never "had the courage to commit suicide," in spite of the fact that thought had occurred in her mind for over ten years. She had often said that she wished she had cancer or some other disease from which she could die.

A year later she had improved sufficiently so that she could take a job at a nursing home connected with the hospital. After two months she became depressed, a pattern which began to appear when she became employed and might likely lead toward her ultimate discharge. She adjusted well enough to be taken off all medication and did very well until the fall when she became "twisted up inside" and left her job. Tranquilizers were again ordered.

Two years later her father died. She showed no undue emotional stress. Eventually when Constance had to face this reality, she became upset and angry at her older sister and her therapist.

During 1964 she vacillated between being sick and well. When she showed success in a situation, she immediately regressed to a non-functioning level.

A year later she didn't show any marked change from her previous condition; she showed facial tics and thought people were observing her. She complained continually that her medication wasn't what it should be; she insisted on changes from the medical staff.

During this time she became more paranoid and showed increasing incoherence and irrelevance. These paranoid feelings involved a female nurse. Connie was aware of her homosexual feelings and sexual role confusion. She would not and could not discuss them in any detail. She stated she was "dependent, self-conscious, lonely, insecure, and ambivalent" towards her hospitalization and wondered whether or not her insight into her problem was confusing her more. Her medications were changed and her suicidal preoccupation subsided.

Miss Knight remained essentially the same during the early part of 1967. Then she started sucking her thumb and making facial grimaces. Occasionally she made noises in her larynx and held her breath. She purposefully engaged in bizarre behavior such as placing her mattress on the floor then criticizing the nursing staff because they reported it to the doctor. When the nurses were instructed to pay no attention to her she put the mattress back on the bed.

During the following year she was admitted to a general hospital for an infection of a right index finger. At this time she wrote strange letters to the mental hospital superintendent and her therapist. She sent the superintendent a brass bluebird wrapped in a gauze square. She sent her therapist a penny and a small packet of salt and pepper. She eventually was transferred back to the psychiatric hospital but showed increasing deterioration in her behavior and thinking processes. In the fall, following another change in her medication, it was noted that she was more cheerful and was taking more interest in her personal appearance.

When she returned to the hospital, she was seen in therapy every week and her condition varied from optimism to depression. However, she managed to keep herself usefully employed at the hospital industrial therapy program and had successful home visits. She again became full of ideas for the future. In spite of being hospitalized for almost ten years, she felt ambivalent about leaving the institution but *she planned to do so* "sometime next year."

After a transfer to another ward at her own request, Connie's behavior was more disturbed than usual. This resulted in her being transferred back to her former ward because of her increased ambivalence, undecidedness which was manifested by immobile catatonic posturing and pacing. She had made several statements to the effect that life wasn't worth living but was not felt to be actually suicidal; she had made similar statements innumerable times over the years. However, she agreed to discuss her situation with her doctor, to stay on the ward and not to leave the ward for her industrial assignment for the time being. Her doctor felt that Connie had always had a good relationship with him as well as the nursing staff. She had never deviated from the ward rules before. Privileges were restored as she was considered better and more responsible.

A month later she threw herself in front of an oncoming car near the private hospital.

She was rushed to a local general hospital and then transferred to a larger nearby medical center. On admission she was diagnosed Schizophrenic Reaction, Chronic Undifferentiated Type with a chief complaint of head injury. It was determined that she sustained a fracture of the skull, contusion of brain, subdural hematoma, and severe swelling of brain tissue, a fracture of the pelvis and multiple fractures of the ribs. She had a stormy clinical course for a month before she died.

CONSTANCE KNIGHT

Constance Knight is another so-called "psychotic" suicide. She was called an "ugly duckling" by her family; but she became an efficient and well-liked nurse. She displayed extreme dependency needs but still maintained her nursing skills for several years. When she was thirty-eight she entered a private psychiatric hospital where she repeated her suicidal ideation so frequently that the hospital staff paid little attention to it. Constance finally threw herself in front of a car on the city streets. Her suicidal intent only went unheeded by the professionals taking care of her. None of them seemed to realize that she had the final desperate courage to dispose of herself in the manner which led to her death.

The Psychotic Suicide

Suicide in obvious psychotic individuals is sometimes superficially explained on the basis that the person does not know what he is doing. A cause and effect sequence is implicit in this type of reasoning. The conclusion is always that the individual committed suicide because he was mentally ill. There is little impirical evidence that mental illness "causes" suicide any more than physical illness may be presumed to "cause" suicide.

A study by Farberow, Shneidman, and Neuringer, *Case History and Hospitalization Factors in Suicides of Neuropsychiatric Hospital Patients*[3] concentrated on extracting a number of factors from the case histories of hospitalized neuropsychiatric patients who suicided. They compared randomly selected factors with the same factors in patients who did not suicide. Based on these factors, "a relatively small number of the items which discriminated between the suicides and the controls referred to developmental or early life-history events."[4] The authors suggest two reasons for this: (1) a lack of sufficient information in the records; (2) a lack of the type of information in the records which is relevant to the suicidal individual. Nevertheless, certain distinguishing factors were found. The authors spell these out in detail and their findings can be summarized by stating that ". . . a characteristic pattern among suicides, which has been tentatively labeled the 'dependent-dissatisfied' person, has emerged."[5] This term is interpreted as meaning the individual who places many dependent demands upon those around him but is dissatisfied no matter what is done. He usually is seen as the perpetual "complainer" in a treatment setting. These people tend to make demands in treatment procedures and numerous other requests whether appropriate or not. They eventually irritate personnel and other patients. In a hospitalization setting, the suicidal patient may be "sicker" than those other patients; he may be a person with marked dependence-independence conflicts.

John certainly had a dependence-independence conflict. His marriage only lasted for about two months and then he returned home to live with his mother. He apparently depended on her

---

3. Farberow, N. L.; Shneidman, E. S.; Neuringer, C.: Case History and Hospitalization Factors in Suicides of Neuropsychiatric Hospital Patients in *Suicide*, Gibbs, J. (ed), New York, Harper & Row, 1968.

4. *Ibid.*, p. 192.

5. Gibbs, *Ibid.*, p. 194.

for most of his life since he either lived with her or took a job that would allow him to be near her. The mother seemed to be the only one who could give to his dependent needs and these were exaggerated needs which could never be completely met. Throughout his life he became discouraged and suspicious. He began to complain about others; he also began to complain of various somatic ailments. Finally, at forty-three he wound up in the state psychiatric hospital where he spent most of the remaining seventeen years of his life.

According to the hospital records, he gave no particular clues as to his intention other than that of his life-style which does tend to parallel that of hospitalized psychotics who eventually commit suicide. The only occurrence of import was probably the medication change; it had initial alerting properties. But with no outlet for his dependency needs, John took the final step—he hanged himself.

Miss Knight also showed an early history of dependency needs. She was tutored at home and later attended a sheltered private boarding school. Over the years various feelings of inadequacy built up like about her poor job performance. She felt that others did not sufficiently appreciate her efforts. With her extreme dependency needs, she became an "injustice collector" and, no matter what transpired, she only saw the unpleasant aspects of things.

The reader is reminded that she undoubtedly went to all kinds of trouble unconsciously to call attention to herself complaining of her treatment program, confusion of her sexual role, etc.

Perhaps Miss Knight "protested too much." She had cried "wolf" so frequently that the hospital staff never felt she would actually kill herself. She did finally lead to her own demise by throwing herself in front of an automobile.

Miss Knight's life-history and course in the hospital also bear a strong resemblance to the "model" of the psychotic suicidal individual which was outlined earlier. She certainly was of the dependent-dissatisfied type who placed many demands on those around her.

The authors do not suggest here that these two cases "prove" the work of Farberow et al.[6] but both of these successful suicides present significant features which closely resemble the tentative outline of the suicidal individual who was a patient in a psychiatric hospital. Research in this area warrants further investigation. Better detection, supervision, and prevention of this type of suicide might become possible.

---

6. Gibbs, *Ibid.*

6

THE ANNIVERSARY SUICIDE

PSYCHOLOGICAL AUTOPSY ON
NEIL BARNEY

NEIL BARNEY WAS born twenty-two years ago in a small New England city. He was the youngest sibling in a family of five children. His childhood had been apparently normal. He was born to his parents late in mid-life, his father almost fifty and his mother in her forties. Neil always claimed he was an unwanted child. In any event, he was considered the baby of the family and was somewhat spoiled. He began school at the usual age and was found to be of average intelligence or probably better; finally, when he was sixteen, he dropped out.

When he was fourteen his parents noticed a change in his personality. He became decidedly "less religious but more philosophical" about things. His parents couldn't elaborate on their comment. At the same time he began to have trouble in school and was truant many times. His parents were unaware of his absences from school. They were unaware that he had developed an alcohol problem.

When Neil was sixteen, he was in an automobile accident and had to be hospitalized for several days. The general hospital record noted that he was difficult to manage in the hospital setting. After he was discharged he returned to school. His recent drinking increased according to friends. At this time his parents became aware that "he was getting in with the wrong crowd."

His psycho-sexual history indicated he first had sexual relations at the age of fourteen preceded by an active mastubatory period. When he was fifteen he admitted two homosexual episodes associated with excessive drinking. He denied any homosexual desires and these two experiences seemed only "drug" related.

After he left school at sixteen he was employed as a carpenter.

This was, in reality, a "jack-of-all-trades" job involving roofing, plumbing, etc. His work record was unsteady and he held similar jobs for many months. At home he refused to help with the usual household chores.

At this time he was elected president of his church's youth group. One comment about this was that he acquired this office as a result of his "unbelievable sociopathic manipulative ability."

Neil was first arrested for breaking into a car at the age of seventeen. The court recommended psychiatric treatment. His family arranged for his admission to a private psychiatric hospital. He was diagnosed as a Chronic Schizophrenic and his progress described as "stormy."

He received tranquilizing medications and electroshock therapy. He showed disturbed behavior on the ward. He also left the hospital, went downtown, and overused alcohol. As a result of this behavior, his medications and electroshock treatment were somewhat increased. He eventually showed some improvement and the medications and electroshock therapy were then decreased and finally discontinued. At his insistence he left the hospital to return home. He made it, but in a drunken state. The following day his family returned him to the hospital.

After another month of hospitalization, his family had a conference with his psychiatrist and it was decided that in Neil's best interest he be taken home the next day. On returning home, he ran away to a neighboring state for four months. The family never heard from him and, when he returned, he offered no explanation. The next two years of his life were almost unaccountable by his family. Neil never got into trouble but it was suspected he was "hanging" in with a crowd.

He then married a girl from a neighboring small town. Three weeks later they both went on a spending spree and passed over a thousand dollars worth of bad checks. When the money ran out, they returned home to face charges and both were put on probation and ordered to pay restitution. Their attitude was that they passed the checks because they needed the money for a vacation.

They each obtained employment that was suitable and moved

into a small apartment of their own. A month later Neil's wife went back to her family. Neil continued to see her on weekends and always begged her to come back to him. After six months Neil reported to his probation officer that he was having trouble with his wife. She was then living in a large city nearby. Neil had gone to see her but was not allowed in by her new boyfriend. After this, things went from bad to worse. His family reported that Neil was mixed up with a "bad crowd" and was using drugs. A local doctor recommended that he be sent to a state mental hospital. The family did not accept this. At the same time his wife filed for divorce.

Subsequently Neil stopped working. He began using drugs and attempted suicide by ingesting several tranquilizers. At this point he was sent to the mental hospital. At this admission he was in a dreamy state and he admitted having used marijuana, lysergic acid diethylamide (LSD), heroin, barbiturates, and tranquilizers. He also revealed his attempt at suicide was serious. "I've been depressed most of my life." The first few days in the hospital were marked by evasiveness, hostility, and suspicion. He was noticed manipulating patients and others for his own gain. His manipulative powers were so great that he was able to fool the hospital staff.

He gradually calmed down and was friendly and cooperative while he was maintained on tranquilizing medication. He was eventually discharged from the hospital with a "very guarded" prognosis and he was advised to attend the outpatient clinic; he never did.

During this hospitalization a brother, who was a policeman, visited the doctor with the request that Neil's treatment be kept strict. Later this same brother told the police that Neil was using drugs and requested that Neil be arrested.

About a month after his discharge, Neil was arrested for selling drugs. He claimed a girl who had been in group therapy with him at the hospital had told the police of his drug activities and, as a result, the police were watching him. For this offense he was sentenced to sixty days in jail. When he was released from jail, he swore he would kill himself if he ever had to return to this type of incarceration. He did get a job and lived at home with his parents. Three months later he quit this job for no apparent reason but was able to obtain two other jobs in quick succession.

During this period, Neil reportedly used more drugs than he had ever done before including lysergic acid diethylamide (LSD), methedrine, and heroin. He told various therapists that he started on drugs when a close personal relationship terminated. Neil became so upset that his family doctor gave him tranquilizers; this eventually led to his addiction problem. A local pusher contributed to both Neil's and his wife's drug problem.

Shortly thereafter he became a friend of a man who was connected with a local news media. Neil openly claimed to be an "ex-addict" campaigning against drugs, berating the drug problem. It is somewhat ironical that while viewers and listeners believed his sincerity, he was usually "high" on methedrine while he was broadcasting.

Another bit of irony was that Neil had told the police about some local drug traffic but he couldn't and wouldn't inform on his close friends. By this time he had been socially ostracized by all his peers.

During these months he began dating a girl whom he met one night when he was invited to a friend's apartment to "trip on acid." They began dating and she eventually became pregnant. Neil didn't argue and, in fact, at first seemed happy about it. This girl lived with her parents but she soon moved out and began to live in an apartment; Neil lived with her. Their friends dropped in frequently to use drugs with both of them. One landlord after another threw them out when he became aware of what was going on and they would move on to another apartment.

Both Neil and his girl friend became involved with other drug users, attending meetings, actually group therapy sessions sponsored by a local agency for young drug abusers. Neil was usually "high" on methedrine when he went. In their participation they both asked many intelligent questions. Neil did seem too preoccupied about one thing; he constantly wanted to know if he would "lose his aggies" if he continued to take drugs. It was felt he harbored a phobia that he would become seriously mentally ill if he kept on using drugs.

During the late fall of his death, his girl friend had their baby. Neil not only seemed to resent having to help in taking care of the baby, but he also seemed to resent the baby itself. He was having difficulty with employment because of his frequent encounters with the local police. His common-law wife was working under assumed names because of her involvements with him.

At this time Neil admitted to a friend that he was having suicidal thoughts and was using a great deal of methedrine. He told this friend that his recent car accident was actually an unsuccessful attempt to commit suicide.

Certain events occurred several days before Neil killed himself. A friend, another drug abuser, died from an overdose of drugs. At this Neil told his common-law wife that if he had to go, that was the way "to do it." He also agreed to marry her.

The morning before his suicide, a friend got in touch with him and invited him to go to a university to hear a talk given by a former student of Timothy Leary. One of the reasons for this was to persuade Neil to work at one of the local college campuses on the drug problem. Neil could talk with the students and tell them of the dangers of drugs. The night before the lecture, Neil called his friend to say his car had broken down and he would not keep the appointment.

The day of his death, which was also the day before his twenty-second birthday, Neil stayed around his parents' home until afternoon. He then again called his friend to say he couldn't come to the lecture. Next he went to the apartment where he and his common-law wife resided. He washed and dried the dishes and smoked a few cigarettes. Then he shot himself in the head with a .25 calibre pistol that the couple used for target shooting. When she returned from work, she went into the bathroom and found Neil's body and a note. It read:

"Dear Lover—

I love you and the baby very much, so please take care of yourselves. I love you.

Neil xxx"

In retrospect Neil was a young man who was essentially emotionally immature and unable to adapt to adult responsibilities. On the positive side, he was physically attractive, of average intelligence, and had a charming, winning way about him. On the other side, he would condemn drugs while he himself was "speeding." Underlying this was a vein of isolation and loneliness, a very schizophrenic feature. He had no close friends as a child. He was melancholy in that he felt the absence of affection and probably realized he didn't know how to commit himself to the basic ties of friendship.

Drugs were the final answer for Neil. Whether he consciously chose the eve of his twenty-second birthday to commit suicide or whether this was an unconscious process, we shall never know. In any event, one might interpret this "anniversary" suicide as an indication that he could not see himself going on "another year."

NEIL BARNEY

Neil Barney was a chronically depressed young man who suicided in his early twenties. While his childhood was essentially normal, he underwent a change in his outlook on life at the age of fourteen. He finally decompensated to the point of being admitted to a mental hospital. A teenage marriage was stormy and ended in a divorce after a short time.

Neil then arrived on the drug scene. He was a user, and, probably for his own protection, became an informer. He had met and was living with a girl friend who became pregnant; Neil lived with her off and on. Immediately previous to his suicide, he had another run-in with the police but it seemed to become more public. He could not get a job. He had agreed to marry again. Nevertheless, on the eve of his twenty-second birthday, Neil took his own life.

PSYCHOLOGICAL AUTOPSY ON
LYDIA GRAHAM BICKFORD

L YDIA GRAHAM BICKFORD was thirty-three at the time of her death by suicide. She grew up in a small New England town. Lydia had one sister and two brothers. Her parents separated when she was very young and she was reared in an orphanage. Her father visited her infrequently. Later in life she told her husband her mother was dead as an explanation for her mother's not visiting. This was found to be untrue.

At the age of fourteen she ran away from the orphanage and married a Mr. Balke but the marriage was shortly annulled. Her first child was born when she was fifteen.

Lydia did not complete high school. She married Bertram Dorset who was fifteen years her senior. He was involved in night club musical groups and was in the process of getting a divorce at the time they met. He went into the service and she went with him. She became pregnant but did not tell him right away. He returned to his former wife for awhile but later went back to Lydia. They lived together for seventeen years. Her husband proved to be very domineering and was a heavy drinker. Their relationship was described as being one of a father-daughter nature, rather than husband-wife.

During this time Mrs. Bickford trained to be a practical nurse. In spite of this profession, she became an alcoholic by her own admission. Eventually Lydia tired of seeing the world from the inside of a bottle.

Mr. Dorset sought a divorce and there were several custody battles which Lydia finally lost on the grounds of being an unfit mother. After that she drifted through several jobs. She finally took a job at a nursing home where she met and married the son of the nursing home's proprietors, Glenn Bickford.

Mr. Dorset told Mr. Bickford that Lydia had tried to commit

suicide several times during their marriage. The attempts were always made by the ingestion of pills.

Lydia admitted having a serious drinking problem when she was in her twenties. She reportedly had overcome this problem by herself and was not known to drink for at least a year prior to her death. She had ready access to drugs since she was a practical nurse and relied on these moderately to relieve tension and to sleep. She did not appear depressed but she was constantly discouraged with the situation of her children. She lost some weight but ate and slept well.

Mrs. Bickford was known to be a very hard worker; she was professional in her dealings first and personable second. She was very much respected in her profession and gave no indication of mental or emotional disturbance to her colleagues. She did not mix in much socially but was well-liked. She was also known to be a very honest person, perhaps painfully so, when it came to duties toward her husband and children. She held a kind of loyalty toward Mr. Dorset and their children throughout her marriage to Mr. Bickford. However, she had initially lied to Mr. Bickford about how many children she had, about her mother's being dead, and about her being married only once. The truth about these matters came out in bits and pieces which she eventually told of her own accord.

One of the characteristics that Mr. Bickford especially enjoyed was his wife's usual sunny, bright, and energetic approach to life. He said, "It would make you feel good just to see her." She was a person who strived to better herself. She frequently bought medical books and studied them faithfully. In fact, in the autumn of the year of her death, she had planned to return to her formal education. She took life seriously and was a planner. On her days off from work, she always had lists of things to do and organized her time accordingly.

Mrs. Bickford always had a steady and predictable nature. Frequently she was placed under stress in her work. She took time to think things through and sought counsel with friends and authority.

However, all was not "sunny" with Lydia, as she had a complex marital situation. Mr. Dorset, her second husband, had remarried and the new Mrs. Dorset reportedly could not get along with the children. As a result of pressure from her, Mr. Dorset allowed the children to go live with the Bickfords. This happened about eight months prior to Lydia's suicide.

Once the five children were with the Bickfords there was an immediate financial problem. Mr. Dorset was not reliable with his support payments for the children and Mr. Bickford had five children of his own for whom he was also paying support. Finally Mrs. Bickford's and Mr. Dorset's children were returned to live with the Dorsets. Mr. Dorset had custody and wished to avoid legal proceedings.

This action really upset Lydia who was unsure of where to live: either with her children and Mr. and Mrs. Dorset, or with Mr. Bickford. As a result of this confusion, the Bickfords sought counsel from their minister and a trial separation followed. Mrs. Bickford moved into the nursing home where she worked. Even then she was in daily contact with Mr. Bickford and telephoned her children very frequently. However, at the end of the trial period, Lydia decided she and Mr. Bickford should seek a divorce.

Lydia moved back in with Mr. Dorset. Just what happened to the second Mrs. Dorset at this time is unclear, but one thing is certain; she had very little influence on Mr. Dorset, Lydia, or the children. After moving back with Mr. Dorset, Lydia realized she had made a terrible mistake Mr. Dorset was still drinking and she said, "Everyone has gone off somewhere . . . I will end up right where I started from."

She went back to live with Mr. Bickford and the divorce proceedings were dropped. Shortly after this reconciliation, she became concerned about sick benefits on her job although there was no apparent sign of illness. Nevertheless, she left her job to work for the telephone company.

The day before she died, Mrs. Bickford had attended her eldest child's high school baccalaureate accompanied by her husband. After the service they proceeded to her daughter's residence which was at the home of an aunt. This was in the same town where Mr. Dorset lived.

As they were walking down the street, the son who had gone with his mother to the baccalaureate spied one of his brothers, Albert; he ran to greet him. As they talked, Mrs. Bickford came up and asked who was taking care of Albert. He replied that he and his brother were taking care of themselves. She asked where their father was and Albert said his father had gone to see his first wife in Florida. As an after-thought the boy added that he had gone for oranges. Mrs. Bickford then said something very much out of character for her, "I'll bet he hasn't gone for oranges; it is probably cherries!"

She was very angry and quietly fumed all the way home. She went almost directly to bed, asking Mr. Bickford to join her. She said that she needed him, and they made love.

The following day she was dead from an overdose of barbiturates.

Mrs. Bickford left a suicide note. The actual note, unfortunately, is not available for reprint. However, its contents expressed feelings that she was a failure as a wife to Mr. Bickford. Another factor which immediately led up to her suicide was that she felt so ambivalent towards Mr. Dorset. She seemed unable to leave him even though he disappointed her on so many occasions. On the other hand, she felt unworthy of having a husband as good as Mr. Bickford. Through all of this turmoil, her suicide eventually evolved.

Mrs. Bickford's body was discovered by her husband when he returned from work. She was stretched out on her bed as if sleeping. Her hair had been carefully combed and their wedding picture was nearby as though it had slipped from her hand. As mentioned above, she left a note to her husband which expressed her love for him and remorse that she had failed as a wife and that she was "born to lose." Lydia had signed it with "All my love" and a pet name. She also left the deeds to two pieces of property she owned, along with a handwritten will leaving her property to her eldest child and only daughter. It would seem that she could no longer decide between which of her "two families" to give her allegiance.

PSYCHOLOGICAL AUTOPSY ON
GLENN BICKFORD

GLENN BICKFORD LIVED to be thirty-four before he committed suicide. He was the second of four sons. His mother is said to have been a "warm person" and operated a nursing home for the elderly for a number of years. His father was somewhat different and was described as "vituperative" as a person. When he said something he expected that it would be carried out immediately.

Glenn's early life was rather barren in that his educational career ended after his second year of high school. About the only other thing known of his early life was that he was shy. This undoubtedly led to his dependence on individuals when he became an adult.

One of his brothers, Eric, seemed singled out to be Glenn's opponent in life. This brother was the better and stronger of the two; the two were friendly enemies and constantly competed with each other. Eventually they ended up living next door to one another in adult life where the rivalry continued. Also, Eric was an electronic engineer; Glenn worked in a shoe shop. Eric's marriage was a success; Glenn's was not.

Shortly after leaving school at the age of eighteen, he obtained his parents' consent to marry. This first marriage was a stormy one and ended with his wife's leaving him after about seven years of marriage. By then they had five children, all of whom went to live with their mother when she left Glenn. The details of this broken marriage were never fully uncovered but Glenn finally divorced her on the grounds of desertion.

Shortly after this, he married for a second time as did his first wife. He had met his second wife, a licensed practical nurse, at his mother's nursing home. This woman, Lydia Graham, had five children of her own. They lived with their own father. Lydia worried about them continually and kept in contact with her first husband, even going back to live with him and his new wife, following her second marriage. Glenn only allowed this because he wanted his wife to be happy. For a while Lydia's children came to live in the Bickford household; this must be viewed in the context of Mr. Bickford's supporting his five children at the same time. This confused alliance between the two families was terminated only by Lydia's suicide after ten months of marriage.

Her suicide served as the last blow to Glenn and he began thinking about his own self-demise. As is so frequently the case, the family was able to see clearly what was going on only in retrospect. Shortly after Lydia's death, he began to think he was being followed. He confided to his minister about this ideation. As a result, the clergyman friend took Glenn to his parents' home. They calmed him down but there was evidence of a continuing paranoid thinking.

When Glenn gave information to the field consultant for his wife's psychological autopsy, he verbalized a wish to be with her at the time. This clue did not go unnoticed. The consultant advised him to seek help for his own problems and frequently, while driving past the home, wondered what was happening in Glenn's life.

His overall personality pattern began to undergo a change. He had always been considerate and hard-working but able to tolerate only minimal stress.

On Memorial Day, approximately a year after his wife's death, Glen went to the cemetery where she was buried and thoroughly cleaned it up. This occurred only three days before his own suicide. Whether this was a portent of death or only one of respect is only a matter for speculation. The following day he telephoned his mother and told her to get in touch with his attorney to see that his final papers were in order. Later he brought a suitcase to his parents' home telling them that everything they would need was in it. He left a payment book for a television set on top of a table. He had threatened by telephone that he would kill himself. His parents had told a friend who was living with him temporarily to call them if anything unusual happened. This man failed to report that Glenn was restless at night for about a week before he died and that he also went out with a gun at least two of those nights.

As the day of his suicide approached, there were several factors which were felt to be upsetting to Glenn. His job had become increasingly unsatisfactory both for his employer and himself. He had become upset that the stepfather to his own children was drinking excessively and perhaps not using the support checks wisely. As the anniversary of his wife's death by suicide approached, he was noted to become more and more preoccupied with her suicide. He began to stay up much later than usual and carried a gun with him. He became temperamental and uncommunicative with family members.

Finally Glenn shot himself in the same room where his wife killed herself—three days before the anniversary of Lydia's suicide.

The Anniversary Suicide

When one attempts to give a typology to suicides, there is an overlap, as the reader quickly recognizes. An "anniversary" suicide may show many clinical clues to the "well-planned," etc., but the fact that the death occurs on an especially significant date makes it a worthy special category.

There obviously is a particular "type" of suicide which has been labeled the "anniversary" suicide. This term refers to the fact that someone commits suicide on an anniversary which is significant to him, such as a birthday, wedding anniversary, or other important day. There is practically no information in suicidology literature about this type of death except its recognition. It is an area in need of research; little completed work is available at this time. Admittedly it is difficult to make many comments about the anniversary suicide since so little has been done. Certain relationship seem obvious without attempts to make detailed interpretations. One meaning is that the individual cannot face the anniversary "date." In Glenn Bickford's case it was the unhappy memory of his wife's death. This was a case where suicide begat suicide. Why would he plan his own demise?

Neil had been diagnosed as schizophrenic. Both men had in common the presence of a mental disorder of the schizophrenic type. Both were rather dependent people. Neil had realistic reasonings for deep sadness. Both men were divorced; for each, first marriages resulted in divorce. Both of these men were quite opposites; but at heart they were depressed and angry men and likely psychotic.

Special comments must be added about the relationship between Lydia and Glenn Bickford. The Bickfords were an unusual couple in that Mrs. Bickford's children lived with her former husband and Mr. Bickford allowed his wife to live, at various intervals, in this other household. This type of unusual, almost bizarre course of events eventually led up to both partners' suicides. Lydia was much loved by Mr. Bickford, but she was a mixed blessing to him, or so it would seem. After her suicide Mr. Bickford began a downhill course. The first reported sign was that Glenn began to think that he was being followed. Glenn's parents and minister managed to calm him down but it is most likely that his paranoid thinking continued.

A psychological autopsy was done on Mrs. Bickford, with Glenn cooperating. At the time of the autopsy, he voiced a wish to be with Lydia. The consultant doing the autopsy immediately advised him to seek professional help.

From that point Glenn drew closer to suicide; he did not seek help. He could tolerate only minimal stress. On Memorial Day, a year after his wife's suicide, he cleaned her grave. He told his mother to get in touch with his attorney to see that his papers were in order. He threatened to kill himself. Glenn's own children were living with his first wife and Glenn had reason to believe that the stepfather was drinking heavily and not caring for the children properly.

As the anniversary of his wife's death approached, Glenn's actions became foreboding. He carried a gun with him. Finally, he shot himself just three days before the anniversary of Mrs. Bickford's death.

7

THE MID-LIFE SUICIDE

PSYCHOLOGICAL AUTOPSY ON
MYRA KENT

MYRA KENT WAS born in a small New England city fifty years ago. There were two brothers and two sisters whose ages are unknown; the family was reticent to cooperate in an interview concerning Mrs. Kent's death. Mrs. Kent was a life-long resident of the place where she was born; she was a practicing Catholic and a member of a Catholic ladies' society. She married Ralph Kent, a skilled laborer, when she was twenty. Two years later their first daughter was born. The first daughter grew up, married, and left home; the second daughter graduated from high school and went on to college.

Myra's father was described as a nervous person and very quiet. She was thirty-four when he died of "hardening of the arteries." His death didn't unduly upset her since she was closer to her mother who was described as a "jolly, wonderful person."

Twenty years before her own death, Mrs. Kent wrote to a clinic for an appointment with a complaint of falling hair. She was seen by a dermatologist who diagnosed the condition as being seborrheic dermatitis of the scalp. Six months later she was seen again and then continued to correspond with this doctor regarding her hair problem for the next six years. When she went back to the clinic toward the end of the sixth year, her chief complaint was that "my marriage is on the rocks." Her husband was drinking. She said her husband had been giving her less attention and spent little time with her. He drank nightly until he was intoxicated; he was going out with other women. She considered herself as working hard to maintain the family and care for the children. No help had been received from "nerve medicine" she had taken and she was at her "wit's end." The reason she requested another appointment was that "my husband stayed out all night until 8:00 A.M." When he returned, he told her he would only give her money for food and would have nothing else to do with her from then on. She stated, "I don't want to break up the marriage if it can be patched up." Her hair was falling out; she had a "lump in my throat," a "knot in my stomach," and had suffered a fifteen pound weight loss in three months. She was diagnosed at this time as Anxiety Reaction in a dependent person with a bad situational problem. She made an appointment with a psychiatrist but did not keep it.

During the next seven years she made seventeen visits to the clinic. She complained of being tense, nervous, having headaches, and falling hair. At one point she was given phenobarbital. Along with the eventual clearing of her skin, she became depressed and was placed on chlordiazepoxide. After that she made five visits in the space of one month to the dermatology department at the clinic.

Three months later she contacted the clinic for an appointment when her menses ceased. Another appointment two months later revealed increasing symptoms of anxiety plus the somatic symptoms related to her anxiety and depression about the past years.

In the summer of the same year, her mother died of a heart attack. This was a great blow to Mrs. Kent since she was very dependent on her mother. In fact, she asked her mother's advice about almost everything. After her mother's death, her feelings of depression and anxiety increased to almost psychotic proportions. She continually wondered how she would be able to take care of herself if anything happened to her husband who was only giving her money to live on. The youngest daughter was leaving in a year to go to college. In view of her poor marital relationship, she became depressed thinking about her inability to cope with life.

About a year later, during what seemed to be a severe anxiety attack, she contacted her family physician and was finally hospitalized for the first time in a general hospital. He prescribed chlordiazepoxide, 10 mg., three times a day, chlorpromazine, 10 mg., three times a day, and butabarbital sodium for sleep. She showed no improvement while hospitalized. A psychologist at a local mental health clinic was asked to see her. She was seen later that same month. Mrs. Kent expressed concern about the appointment to the psychologist because she felt for certain that she would be sent to the state mental hospital. When she was assured of confidentiality, she repeated again that she was worried about her husband's alcoholism, her daughter's going away to school and leaving her alone—especially since she felt unable to take care of herself. Her dependent needs were very obvious during the interview when she asked advice like a small child. She was quite thin and said she had no appetite.

The clinic arranged a psychiatric evaluation the next day. In addition to the above, Myra told the psychiartist she had always enjoyed working but now this had become an added burden. She had worked for sometime in a local clerical position. She still felt her hair was thinning. She became anxious when visiting her married daughter, and when she was in church, and when she did something "unusual;" she added that "my hands and feet always feel frozen."

She further told the psychiatrist that she had had anxiety and depression for at least twelve years. Since her mother died she had been having episodes of anxiety which she referred to as a "wave" coming over her "like a mental block," during which time she had difficulty concentrating or carrying on a conversation with others. At these times her heart beat fast, she had a tight feeling in the back of her head, and she had noted at times a visible tremulousness. The preceding two months she had had difficulty swallowing, her appetite had diminished and she had lost about ten pounds.

In addition, Myra's sleep pattern changed such that she couldn't fall asleep; she lay awake and worried about her daughter's driving, having a steady boy friend, and fearing she might become pregnant—even though the daughter had given her no real reason to be concerned. She was also preoccupied that her own amenorrhea might signify that she herself was pregnant, although she had had no sexual relations. She had a sensation of a "ball in my abdomen" as well as a sensation of "bloating" which reinforced her worry about being pregnant.

During the past year she had wept frequently for no apparent reason; she had found little pleasure in anything and sometimes felt like "giving up." She steadfastly denied any suicidal thoughts when asked by the psychiatrist.

She went on to tell the psychiatrist that when her husband drank she felt she had to agree with what he said or there would be an argument. The psychiatrist felt on the other hand that she was minimizing the extent of her husband's drinking and the stress which resulted from this.

Mrs. Kent had shown, also, a marked decline in her energy level and had had a great deal of trouble keeping up with her housekeeping. The lack of energy tended to worsen in the afternoon. When the doctor suggested that her husband be brought in to talk over their problems, Myra insisted that none of her concerns about pregnancy or statements about his drinking be mentioned.

When this interview finally occurred, the possibility of psychiatric hospitalization was discussed with the couple. It became evident that she could not be maintained on an out-patient basis. She had the potential for decompensation and for an outright psychotic depression. She was diagnosed as Involutional Psychosis, Depressive Reaction, potentially psychotic. She was placed on nortriptyline, 10 mg., four times a day for five days, then 25 mg. four times a day, thioridazine, 25 mg. three times a day, plus 100 mg. at bedtime.

She was seen one week later and then followed up by telephone consultations for the next four months. During this time she showed progressive improvement and returned to her part-time work. At the time of her last professional contact, her medication was thioridazine, 50 mg., two times a day, and nortriptyline, 25 mg., four times a day. She was told to remain on medication for three more months and to return to see the psychiatrist in one month.

In retrospect it is only possible to guess that with the impending Christmas holidays, as well as her psychiatric problems, she fell prey to the "afternoon blues." Mrs. Kent's problems became too much for such a dependent individual; perhaps the improvement provided by the medication gave her just enough energy to end her life on Christmas Eve.

As best as can be determined, Mrs. Kent worked for half the day of her death. She visited a neighbor on that day a little after 1:00 P.M. and asked to borrow his .22 revolver. She said she wanted to use it to do away with a dog that had been hit by a car. The neighbor stated he was busy decorating the Christmas tree at the time and didn't think much about it. He gave her the gun and nine cartridges. Myra's daughter left the house at about 1:00 P.M. to visit some friends and Myra was alone from that time on.

About 4:00 P.M. a friend of Mr. Kent's called him at work about a parcel he was unable to deliver since he could not reach or contact Myra at home. When Mr. Kent arrived home from work shortly after 5:00 P.M. he was unable to find his wife immediately, but as he looked further, he found her in the cellar where she apparently shot herself. "She was slumped in a near-sitting position, clad in low brown shoes, stockings, and a light black dress with brass buttons." Death was determined to result from a gunshot wound of the head and was labeled suicide by the medical examiner. No suicide note was found.

One would logically assume that Mr. Kent would feel guilty about his wife's death because of the stress placed on her by his alcoholism and extra-marital affairs. This is somewhat supported in that he declined to discuss his wife's death and would not see a professional interviewer. In addition, neighbors stated Mr. Kent did not mention his wife's death to anyone.

MYRA KENT

Myra Kent is another example of an individual who was excessively dependent. Her husband had an alcohol problem and he was having extra-marital affairs. She worked hard to care for the house and children.

She herself recognized that she had a problem and went to a mental health clinic for help. Medications seemed to give only temporary relief. She had a genuine seborrheic dermatitis which probably did not add to her own image.

At the onset of her menopause, she made another appointment with the mental health clinic. At about the same time, her mother died. This was a great blow because of her dependent need on her mother. She returned to the mental health clinic where she ventilated her feelings of inadequacy. She was also depressed and anxious. She was placed on other major tranquilizers and anti-depressants. Possibly these gave her just enough energy to end her life the day before Christmas.

Nothing seemed to assist her with her "mid-life" mental condition. Her underlying and most likely unconscious hostility is reflected here; what a way to precede a happy, joyous occasion for her family. One author, G.D.N., knows of a suicide when the victim left the family dining room on Christmas Eve and shot himself.

For some reason she chose a "masculine" way of suicide not really fitting with her character. Perhaps shooting herself was her one last moment of assertiveness in her life.

PSYCHOLOGICAL AUTOPSY ON
ALICIA DUPUIS

ALICIA LATOUR DUPUIS was born in 1916 in a sprawling farming community in a French-speaking section of Canada. She was the third of ten children. She had one older sister, an older brother, three younger brothers, and four younger sisters. All the family was actively engaged in dairy farming. In addition, the father owned and operated a soda bottling factory. Alicia completed six years of education and then stayed home to help with the house and farm work. During this time she worked very hard in her mother's home, many times getting up at 4:00 A.M. to start the family washing, since her mother was not well.

Alicia and her future husband went together for about two-and-a-half years prior to their marriage in the late thirties. Mr. Dupuis described the family as being very close and one of which he was proud to be a part.

Although the family made their home in Canada, they eventually migrated to northern New England. In spite of Alicia's social deprivation problems, a married brother was graduated from medical school and did his residency in psychiatry. Another brother worked for the Canadian Government; and another younger sibling completed one year of law school. These brothers had received their education in Canada at seminary schools. They were away from home during their latter six years of school. Younger sisters were still in school and living at home.

Alicia was a very religious woman and went to Mass several times a week. She told her children they were Communists when they were older and rebelled against going to church more than once a week. She was a fastidious homemaker and a devoted wife and mother. She always attempted to have her home clean; she always gave her children and husband whatever they needed or wanted. At the same time she was never known to buy anything for herself. She was frugal and always had been. Mr. Dupuis had never cashed a pay check or done any of the weekly shopping during their marriage. Alicia would walk miles to shop where she could get bargains on food and stamps. On the other hand, she was very generous. The education of her sons required a large sum of money. If family members asked for such things as sports equipment, she would buy the best she could find; yet she would deprive herself to give to others. After her death it was apparent she was always fearful of being without money. At this time the family searched the house for clues to her suicide and found a sizeable amount of hidden money; they even found money rolled up in a window shade.

Mrs. Dupuis was a very timid and shy woman and she liked to visit friends only in the company of her husband. She also liked to have friends and relatives visit them. Two winters before her death, she had accompanied her husband in taking eighty hours of instruction in improving their English but she never attempted to speak English even in the presence of close friends.

She was always a worrier. She was described as restless and a rapid worker. She became a close friend of the wife of her husband's best friend. She often confided in her and seemed depressed. As her friend stated, "It was often difficult to cheer her as she was always depressed." At no time would she allow her children to tell her husband how she felt or what she worried about. Always in his presence, she attempted to be cheerful and dutiful.

She was sensitive but not really suspicious. She did not get involved with anyone if she felt she would be upset by them. The family did not have much of a social life but her husband played golf weekly and, in the winter, he bowled. The winter before her death, Alicia accompanied him while he bowled but did not participate. She did read, knit, and watch television.

Four years before her death, Alicia was apparently well but decided she would like to reduce her weight. At that time she weighed about 165 pounds. She obtained some "diet pills" and lost twenty-five pounds. She also began to complain of being over-tired and of pain in her stomach. She had been hospitalized three years before for a supposedly bleeding ulcer for which she took antacid prescription. She revealed a fear of having cancer. Her family physician reassured her at the time that she did not have cancer. She never spoke of it to him again. It was believed she had had a fear of cancer for many years, with the diagnosis of having an ulcer.

Mrs. Dupuis was having a great deal of discomfort in her ankle the fall of 1967 and a close friend accompanied her to see an orthopedist. The doctor prescribed phenylbutazone and recommended she return within three weeks to have the necessary blood work done. Members of the family stated she took the medicine for about five months. At the same time she continued on the anti-ulcer prescription and diet that had been prescribed.

Early in 1968 she complained of visual disturbances, shortness of breath, and fatigue. Usually within an hour after eating, nausea and vomiting occurred.

After considerable persuasion by her daughters and husband, she finally returned to her physician who knew her history of a stomach ulcer. Her previous medication was discontinued, but since she was very anxious, trifluoperazine 2 mg., three times a day was prescribed. Prior to her death, she did not return for a check-up as had been directed.

The last two or three weeks of her life Alicia became fearful of being alone and she would request one of her daughters to remain at home if her husband was not there. She was despondent and would not hear what anyone said to her, even in the presence of close family visitors. She was a woman with symptoms of chronic depression and anxiety. At this time she seemed to cling to her religious convictions which enabled her to function.

During the last three to four years of her life, Mrs. Dupuis' menses became irregular and the last year, none at all. She complained of "hot flashes" regularly and also, at times, heart palpitations.

Two to three weeks prior to her death, Mrs. Dupuis continued her daily activities within her home, was able to do her weekly shopping, and to attend Mass three to four times a week. She also worked two hours each day, Monday through Friday, doing housework in a nearby church rectory.

During this same time a daughter frequently found her mother reclining on the den sofa. She was eating only toast and drinking coffee; she lost an additional five to eight pounds. She often cried and during this time she also became agitated. She was irritable and argued more with her husband than in the past. He was a strict father and when Alicia felt he was too strict with their daughters, she more frequently came to their defense and interceded—and usually successfully. There had been few arguments in their marriage for these reasons before this time.

On just one occasion could Mr. Dupuis remember a suicidal threat. One evening he jokingly talked of their future and plans of a trip for them to the south. He said he would enjoy this trip but he commented that he might die before then. She remarked, most emphatically, that he would not be the first one to die.

In the early morning of the day of her death, Mrs. Dupuis awakened her two daughters, Marie and Jeannette, in preparation to go to work. They both had part-time jobs at a local hospital and were to leave the home about seven o'clock when working the day shift.

While her daughters ate a hasty breakfast in the kitchen, Mrs. Dupuis returned to bed in the bedroom next to the kitchen. The daughters noticed that their mother was breathing "heavy" and they questioned her about it. They offered to stay home from work but their mother told them it was just "her heart" and she would feel all right after resting a while longer and that there was no need for them to miss work. They accepted their mother's reassurance and left for work.

Her husband was asleep beside her but he did not hear this conversation. He awoke a half-hour later, got up, and dressed for a day of golfing. He spoke to his visiting son, Robert, and a girl from Canada he had brought home for the weekend. Mrs. Dupuis arose again and prepared breakfast for her husband, son, and his girlfriend. The conversation among the four of them was light and pleasant and centered around the plans for the day. The three left the home in another hour, picked up Mr. Dupuis' close friend and golf partner. They drove to a town about thirty-five miles away to play golf.

Alicia apparently washed and dried the breakfast dishes, made the beds, and straightened out the house. The youngest daughter awoke about mid-morning and had breakfast.

Afterwards Mrs. Dupuis asked her to go downtown, a few blocks away, to buy film for a camera, and requested her to return home quickly and alone.

The daughter returned home in about a half-hour entering the house by way of the back entrance to the kitchen. She went through the kitchen into the next room, a den, and found her mother on the floor in a massive pool of blood. She had stabbed herself in the neck with a nine inch kitchen carving knife.

A piece of beef was cooking on the stove and vegetables were sliced and diced in water to add at an appropriate time in preparation for a stew.

An investigation by the local medical examiner and county attorney led to the ruling of the death as a suicide. Alicia had slashed her throat deeply on the left side using her favorite knife, a nine-inch slicer. She had been using this same knife in preparing the stew.

ALICIA DUPUIS

Mrs. Dupuis was a compulsive "over-performer." She kept her home spotless and denied herself many things. She wanted her children to have everything. She was a very religious woman and that probably kept her going for some time. Alicia was also shy, withdrawn, and restless. One friend identified correctly that she was depressed. She was also a very dependent person. She undoubtedly thought she had cancer. She had some genuine physical difficulties but not cancer. She was experiencing menopause and this was another stepping stone towards her suicide. Mrs. Dupuis had a very low frustration tolerance. The only known overt clue to suicide was that she had stated she would be the first to die. She had a deep well of aggression but was unable to draw on it except to turn it against herself with a knife she frequently used to glut her family's palate.

Mid-Life Suicide

In common, both Mrs. Kent and Mrs. Dupuis had a strain of excessive dependence. Conversely, they were both independent when it came to the domain of household chores. Each of them were experiencing difficulties of a menopause period. In each case it is difficult to assess exactly what the role of the menopause was. But as is so well known from clinical histories, the "change of life" usually plays a significant part in depression in women. Both physical and psychological factors are important. When menstruation ceases, a woman has a markedly different self-picture; she sees herself as having lost something significant in her life. A sign of her femininity has been lost.

Both of these women were depressed and had physical ailments which concerned them. As the psychological autopsy showed, Mrs. Dupuis' depression initially was not so detectable as Mrs. Kent's. It took close friends and family to realize that Mrs. Dupuis was depressed. Mrs. Kent's depression was much more obvious. With regard to medical problems, Mrs. Dupuis had had a fear of cancer for a number of years. This fear was not evident in Myra. It is a well-established fact that cancer-ophobia often plays a significant part in the life history of a person who eventually commits suicide. Mrs. Dupuis did have a history of an ulcer which may have reinforced her fears of cancer.

There are certain stepping stones to suicide which appear to be common to both of these mid-life depressive suicides:

1. Excessive dependence upon the family members.
2. Substantial physical problems with an exaggerated response to them.
3. Depression.

Regardless of whatever help each sought and the aid given, nothing seemed to meet their needs.

8

ELDERLY SICK SUICIDE

PSYCHOLOGICAL AUTOPSY ON
ALBERTA GRANT

Mrs. Grant was the youngest sibling in a family of four children. She was sixty-eight at the time of her death. The family was described as close and stable. Mrs. Grant's father was a publicly known person. He displayed a great deal of affection toward his children and was described as a kind, gentle, and loving person. Mrs. Grant's mother was not so demonstrative in her affections as the father but was also described as a "giving" person. Alberta was closest to her sister, Eunice, who was seventy and living in a home for the aged at the time of her sister's suicide. Another older sister was eighty-six and lived in the same city as Mrs. Grant. Her only brother, Donald, was retired and living and well. This cluster of siblings kept in close touch with one another and there had always been a minimum of friction among them.

Alberta was described as an active child who was friendly and outgoing. Since she was the youngest, she received more attention than her brother and sisters and her childhood was a very happy time for her.

She displayed in her early development a great deal of curiosity and imagination. She was always a leader and a person who was not easily influenced. She attended public schools and was considered a good student. She was active in extracurricular activities and was especially drawn to music and drama. Alberta attended a business school for two years after high school and then worked in a bank. Her job career was short-lived because she met and married Dixon Grant. There were three children born of this marriage.

The marriage was considered a good one but it had its problems. The major source of conflict arose in the form of Alberta's father-in-law. He was described by one of Alberta's

117

children as an "interfering, domineering, son-of-a-bitch." He attempted to run the lives of his son and daughter-in-law.

Although Alberta's husband was often torn between his wife and his father, his father's interference never came close to breaking up their marriage.

The problems in their marriage were not all external. Dixon had a serious drinking problem. This drinking problem never interfered with his work or his family relationships. Alberta didn't have to work during the marriage and she remained a very active person. In addition to being described as a good wife and mother, she was active in various organizations such as the Woman's Club and several ladies' auxiliaries.

After thirty-five years of marriage her husband died suddenly of infectious hepatitis one year after he "licked" his drinking problem. Mrs. Grant took his death very hard. She was overwhelmed but withstood a depression. She suddenly snapped out of this reaction. Alberta then sold the family home and moved into a smaller one. This activity occupied her and seemed to temporarily relieve her stress associated with her husband's death.

She continued close contact with her children and friends. They described her as a loving grandmother who doted on her grandchildren as she did her own. She had learned a lesson from her father-in-law and never attempted to interfere with the lives of her own children. She was described as a liberal and as a person who championed each individual maintaining his own integrity.

She had no romantic interests after the death of her husband and perferred the company of old friends. She spent a good deal of time reading and would sit for hours listening to classical music.

Ten years before her death, Alberta found out that she had Paget's Disease, a bone degenerating chronic illness. This began with a lameness affecting her lower back and legs and it became progressively worse. This lameness was apparently caused by an overcalcification on the ends of the bones; this resulted in a tightening of the joints. She consulted many medical specialists; none could provide any significant relief from this discomfort.

She attempted to keep active but she slowed down as the lameness intensified over the years.

Three years before her death, Alberta suffered a mild stroke. This further debilitated her. Following this mild cerebral-vascular accident, she also suffered a significant loss of vision and this depressed her considerably. She found herself able to read only two to five minutes at a time. In addition, the question of whether or not she should be allowed to drive her car was brought up. She had several minor accidents after this stroke and it soon became clear to her that she would have to give up driving her automobile completely. At the same time, Mrs. Grant had a hearing loss and complained constantly of a roaring in her earns. She again saw otologists but none could help her with this problem.

She sensed that things would get worse. She curtailed her activities and spent most of her time at home brooding. She took various medications, but they provided no relief. Her family said that she was very conservative regarding her medication and never abused it.

Some of her friends seemed to feel that Mrs. Grant drank heavily, but family members felt her drinking was well within normal limits. As far as can be determined alcohol did not contribute to her suicide.

During the last few weeks of her life, Alberta withdrew more and more from social relationships. She found them increasingly difficult and frustrating because of her physical disabilities. The scope of her life was narrowed; physical disability and debilitation were forcing changes in her life which she apparently found intolerable. She was losing an established late life independence.

One fall day she drowned herself in the set-tubs located in the basement of her home. She had written a suicide note, which she mailed to her attorney, telling him where she would be found and detailing her final arrangements that she wished him to make.

Her suicide came as no great surprise to anyone in the family. It was felt, in fact, that the tragedy had already played itself out.

Alberta Grant had always been an active, independent, strong-willed person. In the last few years her activities had to be drastically curtailed because of her physical and medical problems. In her last year it would seem that she saw herself as becoming a dependent person. This would have been the antithesis of her previous life style. It is conjectured that she found this possibility repugnant and unbearable. Taking her life must have been a preferable alternative.

ALBERTA GRANT

Alberta Grant was sixty-seven at the time of her death. She came from an apparently good and above-average home. Her school years were very productive both academically and socially. In fact, for her time, she was more advanced, having attended a business college at a time when women did not often attend college.

She was able to make a more than satisfactory marriage. About the only significant difficulty in her marriage arose from her father-in-law who frequently interfered with his son's and daughter's-in-law marital life. However, they were both able to cope with him and he never posed a serious threat to their marriage. The other main problem in her marriage was her husband's drinking problem, which he finally licked, only to die from infectious hepatitis one year after he stopped drinking.

After her husband's death, Alberta made a good adjustment only to find that she was becoming increasingly ill. First, she had Paget's Disease. That was followed by a loss of vision, then a hearing loss. Eventually these disorders caught up with her and she became increasingly depressed. In particular, she had to withdraw from the active life she once led. Finally, the physical degeneration from which she was suffering became too much and Alberta turned to the unhappy solution of suicide by drowning.

PSYCHOLOGICAL AUTOPSY ON
ROBERTA ISHAM

Mrs. Roberta Isham was a remarkable woman in that at eighty-five she was able to travel by air one evening from the mid-west to the south and then home before she killed herself. That evening she gave little hint of her self-destructive intentions. She washed the supper dishes, packed her belongings, called a cab, went to the airport, and then flew to the deep south to see some friends. At eighty-five she presented a somewhat different picture from other case reports.

Mrs. Isham was a native New Englander from a middle-class family background. She graduated from high school and then became a registered nurse. She did not marry until she was about thirty; at this time in her life, she married another New Englander who owned and operated his own small and successful business. Two years after their marriage, they had their only child, Simon. Rather than bring him up as an only child, a boy from a broken home was taken into the family and was brought up like a son as a companion for Simon. These two boys graduated from high school, attended prep school, and then went on to complete two-and-a-half years of college. At his mother's death, Simon was a disabled alcoholic with an established neurological diagnosis of Multiple Sclerosis. He was considered a "retired engineer." Nothing could be found out of his foster brother. Previously, Simon's father had died at fifty-four of "multiple strokes" which ended in his becoming completely paralyzed.

During World War II Simon's mother returned to the nursing profession, having "retired" to raise the boys earlier. She worked out of a nurses' register and only took nursing services for sick people who had to travel. She accompanied and managed patients who had no families, whatever their destination. She would travel everywhere, register at hotels, and wait for the next case assignment. She had travelled extensively, was young for her age, and attractive. She had become well-known with similar persons as patients. Three of her patients had given her their houses. She sold these immediately at market value. She continued to be financially "well off."

About eight years before her death, she moved to the midwest to live with her son who was not married and who had spent three years building a house there. Eventually the house was taken over by "right of eminent domain." Simon sold out for a profit and he and his mother moved out and went their separate ways.

Mrs. Isham returned to New England to live with a sister-in-law. After she moved in, Mrs. Isham literally "took over" and she became cantankerous and demanding; she was finally asked to leave. This made her very angry. She moved near Simon who also had returned to New England. By this time he was an alcoholic and suffering from a serious disorder. The relationship was not a good one. He visited his mother only when he needed something or to get "what he could scrounge."

During this situation, Mrs. Isham began seeing a general practitioner who was treating her for peripheral vascular disease. She complained that she had pains in her legs. She continually demanded and received more and more medication for the pain. The doctor became aware of her dependency on drugs but continued to give her weekly prescriptions. He felt it was useless to try to wean her away at her age. He was hesitant on the other hand to increase the medication because he was suspicious of a possible suicide attempt. The doctor felt that Mrs. Isham had possibly made several prior attempts but these were unknown as to methodology, severity, or circumstances. Her son denied any previous attempts or even threats by his mother.

Mrs. Isham began a "moving on" to different towns. When she went to a different locality, she would contact a local physician immediately. Each of these usually recognized her drug dependence but also decided to maintain her on medication.

In spite of her "happy-go-lucky" existence, Mrs. Isham was a lonely, depressed woman who apparently saw nothing good or bright on the horizon of her life. She was suffering, either in reality or psychophysiologically, from peripheral vascular disease. She gradually moved closer to her fate. The only noticeable change was that she had increasing visits with her various physicians. She had weekly contact to receive prescriptions and, when these were not sufficient, she would contact him more often or pick another doctor. Although this reaching out on her part did not go unnoticed by the doctors, its meaning was not understood.

The last physician to whom she went attempted to control her glutethimide intake by giving her only a weekly supply. However, she apparently saved it for suicidal purposes.

On the day of her death she was found comatose by Simon. For some reason, he had looked in on her. She was taken to a small local hospital where she died a few hours later. It is interesting to note that she had made plans to have her body given to a medical school upon her death.

Mrs. Isham's death was intentional. Her son did not visit her regularly so she could not depend on his finding her. Because she had been taking drugs for many years, it seems likely she knew how much she could tolerate. But she finally took a medication overdose which brought down the curtain on the black horizon of her life.

Her son commented after her death that "as close as I was to my mother, I knew she'd commit suicide some day." He had taken her medication away from her and had intended going to the doctor; she talked him into giving it back to her. When mentioned that even though he knew she might commit suicide if he returned the pills, he became reticent but then went on to say "she knew she was going to do it."

The night before she took her life, she had on her blue night-dress and asked Simon to get her pink one "which was her best one; I helped her out of the blue one and into the pink one and combed her hair." One wonders if her son tacitly agreed to allow her to commit suicide. After her death he stated, "I knew she was happier because she had a smile on her face and a contented look when I found her. At her age she had had a good life; she had helped many people through their last days and she had no reason to fear death." When asked how he reacted to her death, he replied: "As she would have wanted me to. I am very religious and believe she is happy in heaven."

ROBERTA ISHAM

Mrs. Isham in many ways appeared to be a paradigm of the typical "New Englander." She was fiercely independent, somewhat silent, seemingly aloof, and yet when the need was there, she was always available. She was thrifty and had a canny eye for the dollar and investments.

Her early life appears to have been relatively normal. She married at thirty. Her only son turned out to be an alcoholic with Multiple Sclerosis.

She was a competent nurse who made a career of travelling, escorting her patients throughout the country but, as life began to pass her by, she turned to prescription drugs. This was with the knowledge of her various doctors. She moved from a formerly independent individual to an unstable dependent person who reached out to her doctors for help. In spite of the recognition by both her doctors and son, she successfully "slept" herself to death with prescribed medication.

Elderly Sick Suicide

Both Mrs. Grant and Mrs. Isham were individuals who greatly valued independence. This trait seemingly was part of what eventually led to their undoing. Each of these women was described as being very independent.

Like most excesses of traits, independence is a two-edged sword. When dependence takes the place of independence, it is so unattractive by contrast that the independent person cannot survive for long. This basically is what happened to each of these women in their final self-demise.

Mrs. Grant, unlike Mrs. Isham, had a very short job career. She only worked for a brief time prior to her marriage and then did not work after that. Her marriage was an essentially happy one and three children resulted from it. There were some problems in terms of Mrs. Grant's father-in-law's interfering and her husband had a drinking problem. With her own family

Mrs. Grant had learned not to interfere and took a "live-and-let-live" approach. The development of Paget's Disease plus other debilitating illnesses was the beginning of the end for this woman. Toward the end of her life, she very definitely withdrew and did not associate with people. The reason for this was that her physical problems stood in the way of effective social relationships. All of these together led up to a picture of almost total dependence on others for the simplest needs of her life. It is not very difficult to see that this easily leads to a state of depression and hopelessness. Finally, Mrs. Grant performed the anticlimactic act of suicide.

Mrs. Isham had a similar life pattern. She was a capable nurse and had worked for the better part of her life. As can be seen, she was a true New Englander who was industrious, thrifty, but basically kind. For much of her adult life she had suffered from peripheral vascular disease. She apparently had a satisfactory marriage with one son as issue. Unfortunately, her son turned out to be an intractable alcoholic. For the better part of her eighty-five years, Mrs. Isham had been able to sustain herself but, when illness caught up with her, she was no longer able to go on.

These two examples may come as no surprise to the reader. Each had been active for the better part of their lives and in late life each was struck with a debilitating illness or illnesses. Again the question arises as to why some older people commit suicide and, under similar circumstances, others do not. At first glance one might interpret these two suicides as coming from the cessation of a productive life. However, other older people cease many of their productive activities and do not kill themselves. This problem becomes even more complicated when one sees that the early lives of these two women were thought to be relatively normal. Perhaps this normalcy may be at the root of their problems. Perhaps those who had led relatively normal lives cannot tolerate the contrast of a dependent ailing life. One can see the problem of the elderly sick is not a simple and clear-cut one. Taking the final step may be a simple solution for such an individual.

9

TERMINALLY ILL SUICIDE

PSYCHOLOGICAL AUTOPSY ON
ALEXANDER CAMERON

Alexander Cameron was born fifty-seven years before his death in a small New England town. He was born into a large family with eight other siblings. When he was ten, he sustained a severe head injury from a falling barn beam. Later he also had osteomyeitis in his right jaw bone which finally had to be removed. These two conditions prevented his serving in the Armed Forces; this was a disappointment which his wife reported weighed heavily on his mind throughout his adult life.

In spite of these handicaps, he became an accomplished athlete during his high school years. His interest and direct participation in sports continued throughout the years before his death. He had a special interest in baseball and became a well-respected umpire for twenty-three years in the local non-professional league. Locally he was very well-known and popular in that capacity. He loved athletics and his wife reported he was well-developed, and well-coordinated, and "strong as an ox."

In the late thirties when he was twenty-seven and she was twenty-four, they were married. Early in their marriage he was in an automobile accident from which he sustained another fractured skull requiring two weeks' hospitalization. Following this injury, he began life-long employment as a skilled laborer with a local electric company.

An only son was born seven years after the marriage. When this youth was sixteen, he was killed in an automobile accident; two of the son's friends survived the wreck. This only son was reported as a delicate, thoughtful, sensitive young man. The local community responded immediately to the tragedy by establishing a memorial award for the best scholar-athlete in the local high school. When the son was killed, the mother was shattered and withdrew from the community almost entirely.

129

The father had a more realistic view of his son; he knew that his son "fooled around," such as taking the family car out when he was fifteen. Mrs. Cameron had grown close to her son; they had spent many evenings alone and had comforted each other while the father was out umpiring and also drinking. This drinking had become a problem a few years before Alex's death. After the son's death, Mr. Cameron was hard hit but he did not withdraw. Both parents were totally unable to discuss the event.

The following year, Mr. Cameron began taking sleeping pills regularly. When his physician asked if he were depressed, Alex always denied any such condition. His family physician asked direct questions about suicidal thinking; this always brought a negative response.

Alex always had a congenial relationship with his wife early in their marriage. Later he began working on the power lines at his job and at this time began to hang around with a crowd that drank. His wife noticed that he soon became a regular and heavy drinker. He would come home at an unpredictable hour of the evening and often passed out on the floor.

After his son's death, according to his wife, his alcohol intake increased and he became noticeably more depressed. Sometimes he would stagger home and then two days later his friends would regale his wife with the fact that he had been at their house those evenings for steak dinners and had showed a cheerful disposition. Mrs. Cameron heard that these were wonderful, fun-filled evenings; she never shared them with Alex and his friends. At this time Mr. Cameron resented the fact that his wife would never drink with him; she would have only one drink and then stop.

During this time and also for a great many years previously, his most frequent companion had been a man much older than himself. This man was well-established in the community and was a person who chased a number of women. Mrs. Cameron was sure her husband did not share this latter activity but she noted the relationship between her husband and the older man was of the father-son type. When this man died four years before Alex's demise, Alex was very much grieved. For awhile he treated Mrs. Cameron with more consideration but his alcohol consumption increased. He spent more time at a fraternal club drinking on his way home from work, usually arriving at home before midnight. Friday nights were different; he would remain sober. Usually he played cards and gambled with his friends and wanted to have his wits about him and, more than likely, he came home with money he had won.

During the four years before the death of his close friend, he frequently attended baseball games in New York or Boston. His wife could always predict how he would return. Unfailingly, he came back with an expensive gift for her and a promise to take her the next time. He never kept this promise.

Alex was a man who never finished anything. He started building his home over a score of years before his death but it remained incomplete. Although he did the carpentry work and his wife the painting, the home was never finished. Early in the year of his death, he completed the installation of the new electric heating system in his home which was considered a remarkable job by inspectors. He had begun a summer camp three years prior to his death which was not finished. This had become one of the refuges for his solitary life. Very often, according to his wife, he would go to this secluded area, take long walks in the country following streams and ponds. He often isolated himself at this spot for a weekend. His friends noticed this inclination to be alone and many thought it to be peculiar.

During the summer of his death, Mrs. Cameron began to notice that her husband was very noticeably tired. He didn't seem to have his usual endurance. When she noticed this, she tried to persuade him to give up umpiring baseball games; she was not successful. He had always avoided medical attention whenever he could and avoided seeking professional help at this time. While installing the electric heating system in their home during the winter, he seemed weak. Following that he had an ulcerated tooth and went to a dentist for treatment. He began to gain weight which was described as being "bloated." This condition became severe and he was hospitalized and diagnosed as having nephritis. Both kidneys were found to be almost nonfunctional. His wife was told that her husband would live only three to four weeks. Although Alex wasn't told that his condition was terminal, it is assumed he guessed the same prognosis before he left the hospital in early spring. A request had been made at a Boston hospital for an early appointment to consider a kidney transplant operation. Alex was reluctant about this consultation because of the expense and the operation itself.

When his wife picked him up at the local hospital at the time of his discharge, he was not too depressed. He had been told that he would be able to walk only a short distance downtown but that he would be able to drive his car. Neither of these activities became a reality. His wife thought he began to realize that when he discovered he could no longer button his trousers because of fluid accumulation that he recognized his serious physical condition. He could not button even his topcoat on his enlarged body.

When they left the hospital, the couple drove to a local pharmacy to have prescriptions filled. Alex insisted on doing it himself. Almost before the car stopped, he got out and went into the pharmacy. He was pale and weak and, noting his condition, the pharmacist provided a chair for him. When he arrived home he went directly to bed. He slept and after awakening, he carefully inspected his room and later the entire house. He remarked how happy he was to be home and how much objects in the home meant to him.

During the next five days his wife estimated he was awake for a total of five hours. Many friends came to call but he refused to see any of them. To be more precise, he didn't want any of them to see him.

His teeth had become loose suddenly and when Alex tried to discuss this with his doctor, the physician would change the subject, a tactic that didn't seem to fool Alex one bit but merely confirmed his feeling that he wasn't going to make it. He requested sleeping pills from the doctor. Placebos were prescribed with his wife's knowledge. At a date closer to his death, the request was again made and this time Alex was given real medication.

Alex did celebrate his fifty-seventh birthday and he received more than fifty cards from friends and relatives. He never looked at them. A few days later he did ask his wife to open them and to read to him the name of the sender. Mrs. Cameron attempted to describe the card or read the message but she was rebuffed by her husband. This was done at the kitchen table where Alex sat with his head buried in his arms on the table.

Mrs. Cameron commented after her husband's death that he never cried but that she often noted his eyes were often "filled with tears." She tried to keep her own grief and remorse from him by crying in other parts of the house.

A week before Mr. Cameron's death, a close friend for twenty-three years brought some company insurance papers to be signed. Mrs. Cameron knew her husband would have refused to see him, so she quietly asked him into Mr. Cameron's room. He said to his friend, "I'm not going to make it—I'll never make it to the hospital."

A few days prior to his suicide, Mr. Cameron told his wife where she would find a sum of money and a bank book in the house. His wife followed the instructions, found what he had told her, returned, and remarked that this certainly was strange. Later she revealed that she never would have found these "deposits" had he not revealed them to her.

At this time he told her about a letter he had written to her four years previously which was being held in his sister's safe-deposit box. The letter, written when he was feeling ill and not himself, began, "If this happens as I know it will . . ." The letter further elaborated on the fact he had always been very selfish and inconsiderate of her but that "no one has loved you more than I have." Although very independent during the marriage, he often remarked after his release from the hospital, "Remember, I will pay you for this (care)." He also frequently said, "I never thought I'd see the day when you gave me a bath— I feel just like a baby." It seemed to bother him very much that his wife, a nurse's aide, had almost to totally take care of him.

Four days before he died (a Saturday) Mr. Cameron went to see the doctor. Both had received letters from the hospital saying he would be admitted for a kidney transplant in a month. Both his family doctor and Alex had hoped he could be admitted immediately although he was concerned about the surgery and expense. Mr. Cameron, recognizing his critical condition, wondered why it wouldn't be possible to go to the hospital right then. His doctor said he would call the hospital the following Monday, to which Mr. Cameron queried that if his condition were so critical, why didn't he call then. He left the doctor's office and returned home; he was obviously depressed. Immediately he went to bed and rested for three or four hours. He then asked his wife to take him for a drive. They drove around for about two hours and he insisted that she not go more than thirty miles per hour. Mr. Cameron's only remark during the entire trip was, "We put those poles and lines in," referring to his employment with the electric company.

Two days later Mr. Cameron's sister came over and took him for a drive in his own car. He said, "I want to drive; I don't want to lose my confidence." He tried and was able to drive only four miles when the car wobbled off the road. His sister drove the rest of the way. Alex was exhausted when he arrived home. Later that day he said to his wife, "Tomorrow we'll go to the bank and to the hospital and pay the bill." His wife assured him his hospital insurance would cover the bill, which it did, but he kept insisting.

Several significant observations may be made about events during the next twenty-four hours before Mr. Cameron's death. At this time Mrs. Cameron noticed that when she gave her husband his medication, he stared at the pills for some time instead of popping them into his mouth and swallowing them with water as he had always done before. He just stared at his legs, rubbed them, and sighed frequently. In retrospect she thought he had looked at them as if to say, "This is for the last time." She described a frequent, bewildered expression was on his face and she felt he was absolutely crushed.

Finally, and on the day of his death and very suddenly, he asked and then ordered his wife to go and pay the hospital bill. As was reconstructed, he must have dressed himself, then went to the cellar of the house and cut forty feet from the fifty-foot garden hose and then left the house. When his wife returned home late midafternoon, she arrived coincidentally with

Alex's sister who was making a routine call. They entered the house together. Mrs. Cameron immediately noticed the small medicine tray had two bottles which were tipped over and that the bottle of sleeping pills was gone. At this point she began to feel guilty at having been tricked out of the house. Alex was gone. She went to the basement and noticed the garden hose had been cut. She held out hope that he would be too weak to do anything. The local rescue squad, the fire department, family members, fellow former employees, a minister, and the county medical examiner were immediately notified and a search began. One searcher said, "I'm doing this because he would do the same for me."

The search lasted twenty-three hours until Mr. Cameron was found in the middle seat of his three-seat station wagon, dead from carbon monoxide poisoning; his car was parked at the end of a dirt road. The garden hose had been placed through a rear window on the passenger side of the vehicle; the other end was attached to the exhaust pipe. The ignition key was in the "on" position, the gas gauge read empty and the shift was in neutral. A large rock had been placed on the gas pedal. On the front seat of the car a fifth of brandy was found with three or four ounces missing.

Mr. Cameron clearly intended to commit suicide; the preparations for an execution of the act were carefully made. He was in the final weeks of a terminal illness when he died. He sensed that he was about to die and couldn't bear the rest of his days.

ALEXANDER CAMERON

In spite of this man's external exuberant life pattern, e.g., enjoying people, socializing "normally," etc., Alex Cameron was basically a "loner" and really did not confidently relate to any other person, including his wife. He attempted and actually gave a picture of a very independent person. In fact, he was not. When he became so dependent on his family members, he came to a point where life was no longer endurable. He knew his life was a "chance," like the innumerable ball games he had umpired. He couldn't risk the outcome and carefully played his own "game," to the final inning.

PSYCHOLOGICAL AUTOPSY ON
RAYMOND ARNOLD

Raymond Arnold was an eldest child who had two younger sisters. When he reached the ninth grade, his mother had been dead for two years and his father remarried. In his early years he had four stepbrothers and a stepsister. When he didn't get along well with his new stepmother, he left home before finishing the ninth grade of school.

During the next few years he worked at many jobs: milkman, bulldozer operator, baker, meatcutter, paper hanger, painter, etc. He was the type of man who could look at a piece of machinery, a crane for instance, and though he had never operated one before, he could persuade a prospective employer that he knew how to do the job. He would then proceed to function in the job satisfactorily.

When he was twenty he married for the first of three times. This marriage lasted twenty-seven years and finally ended in divorce. There was one son, Andrew, from this marriage. Raymond married again within a year following the divorce and had one daughter from this union. This marriage ended with his wife's death after five years and in the spring of the same year, Mr. Arnold remarried for the third time.

In his late twenties, Mr. Arnold had taken flying lessons and was the airport manager in a medium-sized New England city. Flying was always a hobby outside his business. He eventually returned to the family furniture business.

It was in the midst of the early thirties depression that his company went bankrupt. The creditors demanded immediate payment. This would have dealt an immediate death blow to the company. Somehow Raymond bought the company from his father and faced his creditors with a choice: the creditors could demand immediate payment and get one cent on the dollar or

136

they could extend his line of credit and he would repay each of them in full. Realizing their predicament, the creditors stuck with him and were repaid in full as promised. He remained connected with the company until his death.

Mr. Arnold was actively interested in many community groups and held membership in many local lodges; he was also elected to a state position.

During his life he seemed closer to his son, Andrew, than to any other person. This relationship was mutually enjoyable and Andrew was brought into the company about twenty years ago. He was made a partner and remained so until just prior to his father's death at which time his father sold the entire business to him.

Mr. Arnold was a very out-going man who was described as even-tempered. His wife and daughter never saw him lose his temper: neither had his son with whom he worked daily. He kidded his family and they loved it; he always had an inflection of gentleness and good humor with the family and friends. He never complained and was never temperamental. He was an action-oriented man. When something had to be done or needed to be done, he would immediately tackle it.

He was generous to his family with his material success, yet he didn't over-indulge them. Raymond liked people. Outside the closely-knit family circle, he had a great many friends and was highly esteemed in his community.

In his home and in his work there never was any reported disharmony. He managed his business and his family very well; in both places he was the "boss" and events or situations which might have upset others weren't even noticed by him or, if they were, he didn't show it. His response to problems was to solve the situation simply and quietly even when it meant working harder.

Eight years before his suicide, Mr. Arnold had a routine physical examination. This included an electrocardiogram. These results showed "a silent heart attack." This information was telephoned immediately to his wife and he was immediately hospitalized. During his three months' stay in the hospital, he had two more heart attacks plus a blood clot in his lungs. The doctors did not expect him to live. But he recovered and when he complained that he was going "stir crazy" and wanted to go home, his physicians gave their permission after his wife learned to administer shots of meperidine.

After returning home, his wife administered 50 milligrams of this medication whenever he complained of chest pain. This became more frequent than once a day. For months this situation existed as he spent most of the time on the couch in the living room of his home.

As was customary, the Arnolds left for Florida just before Thanksgiving 1962. His wife and daughter drove down but Raymond flew down because his doctors did not feel he could survive the automobile trip. By the time they returned the following spring, Raymond was administering the drug himself, which included three or four shots during the night while the rest of the family slept. Until the year of his death, his world was his "own little drug world," according to his wife and, in addition, consisted of a couch in the living room which he soon wore out.

A few months before his death, he complained of his eyes. He said they "feel like someone is sticking knives in them or rubbing sand in them." He also complained of his throat which "feels as if it were on fire," and very dry and uncomfortable. This condition seemed to grow worse and two months later he went to a hospital to seek help where he remained six days. No organic basis for his eye and throat problems could be found. His physicians, aware of his addiction, asked him if he would be willing to try to kick his drug habit. When he was informed it would take about two weeks and could not be done at home, Raymond lost interest.

Throughout this period his wife said that she thought he was contemplating suicide. He would frequently say, "I wish I were dead;" "If I had the right kind of pills, I'd do something;" "My God, if I have to live like this, I'd rather not be around;" etc. His wife, son, and daughter decided that he should never be left alone and saw to it from that time forward that he wouldn't be.

His eyes and throat still bothered him and much more so after he left the hospital. He asked his wife, "What shall I do; shall I take the cure?" referring to his addiction. Arrangements were made for withdrawal and during his six-day stay in a local hospital, he went from a full bottle of meperidine each day to nothing at all. The withdrawal didn't seem to be too uncomfortable for him considering the extent of his drug abuse and addiction problem.

He had an appointment with his doctor two days before his death. But Raymond requested and was given an earlier appointment. He was given penicillin for his eye and throat complaints. The following day he requested another appointment but could obtain only a doctor covering for his regular doctor. He was given additional penicillin.

During these two days the Arnolds had a couple visiting them. Raymond socialized normally even though he complained that his eyes and throat still bothered him. His wife noted he generally acted and felt better than he had at any time during the previous six years. His friends later reported to his wife that her husband had mentioned suicide during their visit but they could not recall his statements.

Consequently with his eye and throat complaints, Mr. Arnold felt for the past six months that he had cancer of the throat; no amount of reassurance could dissuade him of this notion. He was dying of cancer and he repeatedly asked his wife, son, daughter, and doctors whether it was true or not. They said no but he didn't believe them. He knew a close friend of his was dying of cancer. He couldn't understand how his friend could continue to live like he did and often expressed this to his wife.

The forty-eight hours before Raymond died are of interest. Seemingly, nothing eventful transpired. At the onset of this time he walked over to a construction project near his home and acted as a sidewalk superintendent. Then he went briefly to his business returning home a short while later.

The next day was also quite usual. He went to the business to help out and actually took care of four or five customers since his son customarily did not come in on Saturday mornings. He seemed happy and fine. He was back home in the late morning but complained of a very sore throat and bothersome eyes. He called his doctor who saw him during the middle of the afternoon. After Raymond asked directly whether he had cancer of the throat, the doctor said "No" and proceeded to order three more prescriptions including lipocaine. Mrs. Arnold picked up the prescriptions at the drug store.

Instructions on one bottle said it was to be taken every two hours and swallowed only if pain was present, otherwise it was to be spit out. He swallowed the first dose. After an hour and a quarter he began to ask for more. His wife held him off for thirty minutes longer and then gave him his medication. This went on for the next three hours. About 9:00 P.M. he was sound asleep on the couch. When his wife tried unsuccessfully a few times to awaken him, she finally got him up and awake. He said that he had taken two sleeping pills. Evidently he had slipped out into the kitchen while his wife and daughter were watching television and had taken the tablets from the medicine tray. She urged him to go to bed but he wanted more sleeping pills. Normally he had chlordiazepoxide, two sleeping pills, and a laxative. After he went to bed, she returned to the medicine tray, removed the chlordiazepoxide and sleeping pills, and hid them in a kitchen cabinet.

Before his heart attack, Mr. Arnold was a fairly heavy drinker. Following the heart attack, he had nothing to drink except once in Florida. He drank part of a bottle and was so ill for two or three days that no one thought he would live. A regular physical examination revealed his liver was in poor condition and an examination six months later indicated his liver was operating at one-third its normal capacity. He was instructed never to take another drink.

Mr. Arnold prepared for his death with the following changes in his life that he initiated four months before he died: (1) He changed his insurance policy beneficiary to his first wife so she could be provided for in the absence of alimony payments; (2) He sold his remaining interest in the furniture store to his son with payments to be made to his survivors; (3) He had an apartment he owned re-roofed and repainted; (4) He purchased a new car for his wife and a new car for his daughter; (5) He had his own home painted and roofed; (6) He made a new will; (7) He made arrangements to have his father's grave receive perpetual care and made full payment; (8) He had the deed to the property where his home is located finally cleared; there had always been some legal loopholes connected with his ownership of it; (9) He established a trust fund for his daughter; (10) He sold two lots he owned in Florida; (11) He took his wife to a hearing aid specialist and ordered a new hearing aid for her (he never would have done this before, his wife said, he would have let her handle it in her own way and in her own time); (12) He urged his daughter to have a cartilage growth on her knee trimmed as soon as possible so it wouldn't bother her throughout her life.

When he went into the store just before his death, he gave directions to some of the employees which was resented. His son said that help was hard to get and they really should have only one boss. Mr. Arnold said, "Well, that's what I get; I sell you the company and you take right over." Andrew took this as he did other kidding which Mr. Arnold had just recently begun again as a good sign and an indication that his father was on the mend. He hadn't seen his father look or act so well in six years as he did near the time of his death.

Between 5:00 and 6:00 A.M. on the day of Raymond Arnold's death, Mrs. Arnold awoke and found her husband seated on the edge of their bed. It was perfectly normal for Mr. Arnold to be up at that hour for ever since she had known him, he arose at that time. She asked him if he were all right and he said that he was. She went back to sleep. About 7:00 A.M. his daughter awoke thinking she heard an engine running. She looked out in the yard, saw no car, and went back to sleep. She hadn't noticed the garage.

About 9:00 A.M. Mrs. Arnold awoke and went downstairs. The coffee had not been made and that was very unusual since Mr. Arnold got up so early and always made the coffee. She heard the dog barking in the yard so went outside thinking her husband was in the backyard or near the swimming pool immediately behind their house. As she left the house, she noticed the garage door was shut. It was an electrically-operated door which he always disconnected in the spring and left open during the warmer weather. She rushed to the small side door knowing he must be inside, already guessing at the circumstances.

He was lying on the floor dressed in his pajamas and a short jacket. His wife returned to the house and called the ambulance and the daughter who was still upstairs. The ambulance arrived with three men, one employed by Mr. Arnold who was also a member of the rescue squad. These men concluded immediately, because of their knowledge of his history of heart attacks, that he had had another. They assumed that since his body was still very warm, he was still alive and immediately began mechanical resuscitation and started to the hospital. It never occurred to them while they were driving him to the hospital that he would be found "Dead on Arrival," or that he might have taken his own life. His daughter had touched his cheek and was sure he was dead before he was placed in the ambulance.

Mr. Arnold clearly intended to kill himself. He left no chance of being discovered in his Sunday morning death. Any other day of the week, men from his company would have been arriving from 6:00 A.M. on. The only possibility was that his wife or daughter might wake up and hear the motor running. His face was only a few inches from the tip of the exhaust pipe and he was directly in the path of the monoxide.

RAYMOND ARNOLD

Raymond Arnold was seriously and almost terminally ill. He was obsessed with the idea that he had cancer of the throat. His real trouble lay in a heart condition and a liver ailment. His suicide was carefully planned just as he had carried out the rest of his business. He set things carefully in order before his own demise. He was calm and normal but nothing his family could say altered his wish for death.

The Terminally Ill Suicide

On the surface it is easy to say that the individual with a terminal illness may have an objective reason for committing suicide. Life has lost its meaning; a long and painful death may await him. But still there are other people faced with fatal illnesses who do not kill themselves and hold out hope that they might be cured or relieved in some manner. For those who do commit suicide, it makes no difference whether the illness has an organic basis or whether it stems from a morbid fear. The illness is just as real in either case.

Alexander Cameron had a serious, life-threatening illness, which would have required a kidney transplant for survival. He was, at one time, given only three or four weeks to live. He was not told how seriously ill he was, but he quickly guessed. He spent much of his time sleeping and refused to see old friends as he did not want them to see the condition he was in. He was even clever about getting his wife out of the house so that he could commit suicide.

Raymond Arnold was similar in personality to Mr. Cameron in that he was thorough and independent. His life was complicated by addiction to meperidine as a result of his illness. However, he underwent a remarkable detoxification and recovered from his addiction. He had cancerophobia. He gave many "cries for help." As a last step he carefully put things together in preparation for his death. His plan for suicide was just as carefully carried out.

EPILOGUE

THIS BOOK HAS been designed to acquaint the reader with various facets and intricacies of suicide as it has actually happened. It may be viewed as a panorama of suicide behavior as reported in New Hampshire.

The authors wish to emphasize that no theory of suicide is presented or implied. The "typologies" are convenient descriptions of various types of suicide which are not meant to be comprehensive nor mutually exclusive. But they do provide a foundation for discussion and question. Hopefully, information in the book will provide a practicum for those interested in the field of suicide prevention, crisis intervention, and other allied programs.

The book is meant to serve students, professional, and lay people. As such, its scope has been broad and technical language has been avoided.

The chapter on Adolescent Suicide was geared toward pointing out the special tragedy of suicide in the young person. Both teenagers came from homes fraught with pathology. For example, Howard Jessop's father was depicted as being not understanding; he was also harsh. While the father was away, the mother reportedly had male companions. A sister was pregnant before marriage. Obviously Howard was aware of these things and became exquisitely sensitive to family problems. Sometimes adolescents respond to these situations in drastic ways.

Young people pose a special problem for suicide prevention in that they cannot usually avail themselves to common modes of crisis intervention. Adolescents are not likely to contact a suicide prevention service even if one is available. This is usually because of not being knowledgeable of the service. Other modes of crisis intervention also are not geared to the young person. Whatever is the best approach remains to be determined.

The chapter on Impulsive Suicide logically seemed to follow the Adolescent Suicide as another facet of immature behavior. The adults who act so impulsively can only be thought of as being explosive and emotionally immature persons indicating signs of serious underlying pathology.

Both of the impulsive suicides came from financially poor homes, like the teenagers in this book. It is interesting that one impulsive person had a long string of petty offenses against the law which suggests a history of a pattern of impulsive acting out behavior. Ted Croft was "more-or-less" the town bum. He had been forbidden by the local police to go to a place where he had caused trouble. He was a drifter and a person without any aims and goals. Albert Boyd fared relatively better, but still was very impulsive.

With respect to suicide prevention, it is difficult to say whether either of these individuals would have contacted a suicide prevention service. Both of their adjustments to life were primitive, and it seems doubtful whether either would have turned to the relatively sophisticated suicide prevention service. On the other hand, both might have responded to a neighborhood drop-in center for help. The impulsive behavior which led to their downfall might have been put to positive use, had their impulsivity led them to a neighborhood center, had it been available.

The Planned Suicide poses a very different question. Both of the persons presented here obviously engaged in conscious and carefully planned demises. The individuals reported were very much different. Miss Frederick was passive and well-behaved; Mrs. Cantel was more social and active and had a promiscuous youth. They both had had a serious mental disorder. However different these two people were as far as mental illness, they both arrived at the same solution to their problem.

Miss Frederick gave few or no "cries for help" in her planned suicide. Mrs. Cantel gave out a number of clues, but they went unheeded. It is reasonable to think that Mrs. Cantel, at least, would have reached out for a suicide prevention service were it available to her. Miss Frederick's possible actions leave one with a question mark. She had many positive features, but her essentially passive personality may well have prevented her from contacting such a service.

Suicide prevention and crisis intervention must gear themselves to the Miss Fredericks of this world. Perhaps less emphasis on telephone services and more emphasis on neighborhood crisis drop-in centers would be more attractive. The drop-in center, once established, would become a natural part of the local community.

The most difficult and puzzling suicide to the authors was that of the Minimum Signal. In this one case presented in the book and so typed, the victim appeared well to his family and associates, but suddenly took his own life. It would be impossible even to suggest what type of prevention or intervention service might be effective for a person of this sort. This kind of suicide does occur and speculations must be made.

Mr. Palmer might well have been helped if some of his contacts were better educated for crisis intervention. The topic of suicide is a matter that professional schools have shied away from until recently. Public education in this area has not dealt with suicide at all. An intensive program for this detection of "cries for help" might have a real impact toward the saving of lives. For example, had Mr. Palmer's attorney been better informed, he might have been better able to provide appropriate assistance. Had the family members been better informed, they might have detected signs of an impending disaster, such as a fear of failure.

The two cases of Psychotic Suicide illustrate that the throes of a serious mental illness probably contribute to the final act of suicide. Both cases were psychiatrically hospitalized at the time of their respective suicides. The authors do not mean to preclude an existing mental illness in the other persons described in this book. In both individuals the implications for prevention of psychotic suicide are complex and not easily sorted out.

A beginning point may be the medication change for John Rogers. This, together with a denial to return to a former hospital ward, appeared to alert him sufficiently to summon the strength to commit suicide. It would seem that with hospitalized patients, the prescribing physician should exercise caution when dealing with medication changes in chronic psychiatric patients. Listening to the patient's thinking and concern must be emphasized. It is so easy to speculate what might have happened if Mr. Rogers had been transferred back to his original ward as he requested.

It is not only in large public mental hospitals that patients can kill themselves. Miss Knight was at a good private hospital; yet she managed to jump in front of a car. Miss Knight's whole life style may be viewed as self-destructive. The ultimate happening was only a culmination of many circumstances. The authors would emphasize that the most important aspect of this case for suicide prevention is never to ignore the patient's threat to commit suicide. Professional persons must not become inured to "cries for help" if they are repeated frequently. In a situation with a life-long history of self-degradation, the "cries" are especially important.

The Anniversary Suicide is a most emphatic, devilish, and hostile occurrence. The husband-wife suicide in our data is most intriguing. Mrs. Bickford's death was such a blow to her husband that he killed himself a year later. A person who would commit an anniversary suicide must plan ahead rather carefully, but the authors separate this type of suicide, recognizing overlaps between their typologies. Suicidologists have recognized 'anniversaries" as critical times. These were not an impulsive act. In each situation it seems that these people would have contacted a suicide prevention service if available. The anniversary suicide problem may be the hardest person to reach. The authors believe that suicidologists should give thought to other suicide anniversary linkages providing services with known contacts at these important dates in the person's life.

The Mid-Life Suicide may possibly be partially explained on a physical basis. It is commonly known that both the menopause and climacteric can be accompanied by depression and feelings of loss and loneliness.

At mid-life an individual often stops to reflect on his successes and failures in life. If he perceives himself as having failed, or not doing as well as he hoped, a serious depression may ensue as was the situation in both of the presentations.

For the Elderly Sick and Terminally Ill, one can see that suicide may often be thought of as a "solution." Those who have had long and painful illnesses, or even the threat of a debilitating illness, such as Alberta Grant had with Pagets Disease, look for a ready "out" from their pain and suffering. Chronic debilitating illnesses carry with them the threat of social withdrawal and rejection of friends. In the Elderly Sick, the transition from independence to dependence is a psychological trauma to the ego. Someone else frequently makes an "important decision," perhaps resisted by the person directly involved.

In the Elderly Sick the only prevention means may be frequent visits from friends and neighbors who may help dissuade suicidal preoccupations by attempting to keep the individual's mind occupied with something other than himself.

The Terminally Ill are the saddest persons to consider. Their lives are due to end and they know it. How to intervene and prevent these persons from taking their own lives is a real problem. Care must be taken not to be too pessimistic, suicide-wise, about terminally ill patients. Most of these patients do not commit suicide.

Whatever the types of suicide one may encounter, the problem and question seems to be the same for all age groups. This does seem to boil down to awareness, education, intervention, and prevention.

From this study the authors would advise that "listening" is of utmost importance, second to providing the recommended services.